CURTIS
MEMORIAL
LIBRARY
A World of Possibility

**Margaret Hall Cole
Fund**

India and Pakistan

Tilak and Gokhale: Revolution and Reform in the Making of Modern India (UC Press)

Nine Hours to Rama

Morley and India, 1906–1910 (UC Press)

An Error of Judgment

Roots of Confrontation in South Asia: Afghanistan, Pakistan, India and the Superpowers

Jinnah of Pakistan: A Life

Massacre at Jallianwala Bagh

Zulfi Bhutto of Pakistan: His Life and Times

An Introduction to India

Nehru: A Tryst with Destiny

Gandhi's Passion: The Life and Legacy of Mahatma Gandhi

Encyclopedia of India (editor)

Shameful Flight: The Last Years of the British Empire in India

A New History of India

India (UC Press)

India and Pakistan

Continued Conflict or Cooperation?

Stanley Wolpert

UNIVERSITY OF CALIFORNIA PRESS

Berkeley   Los Angeles   London

University of California Press, one of the most distinguished
university presses in the United States, enriches lives around
the world by advancing scholarship in the humanities,
social sciences, and natural sciences. Its activities are
supported by the UC Press Foundation and by philanthropic
contributions from individuals and institutions. For more
information, visit www.ucpress.edu.

University of California Press
Berkeley and Los Angeles, California

University of California Press, Ltd.
London, England

Library of Congress Cataloging-in-Publication Data
Wolpert, Stanley A.
    India and Pakistan : continued conflict or cooperation? /
Stanley Wolpert.—1st ed.
        p.   cm.
    Includes bibliographical references and index.
    ISBN 978-0-520-26677-3 (cloth : alk. paper)
        1. India—Foreign relations—Pakistan.   2. Pakistan—
Foreign relations—India.   3. India—Military relations—
Pakistan.   4. Pakistan—Military relations—India.   I. Title.
    DS450.P18W65   2010
    954.04—dc22   2009049420

Manufactured in the United States of America
19 18 17 16 15 14 13 12 11 10
10 9 8 7 6 5 4 3 2 1
The paper used in this publication meets the minimum
requirements of ANSI/NISO Z39.48-1992 (R 1997)
(Permanence of Paper).

To the innocent Kashmiri victims of the deadly
cross-fire between India and Pakistan
over the past sixty-three years.
May peace prevail.

CONTENTS

MAPS

PREFACE AND
ACKNOWLEDGMENTS

No Asian conflict has proved more deadly, costly, or intractable than that which continues to divide India and Pakistan over Kashmir. For the past half-century, since I first became aware of this conflict's potential for regional destruction, I have pondered the alternatives for its resolution. Many wise friends—Indian, Pakistani, American, European, and Australian—have assisted me in understanding the complexity of the conflict.

When I chaired the History Department at UCLA, Rafique A. Khan, a leader of the Kashmiri community in Los Angeles, first urged me to organize an academic conference to explore how to help achieve peace in Kashmir. Prior commitments and obstacles, however, prevented me from launching so ambitious a project until April 2002, when the Ronald W. Burkle Center for International Relations at UCLA agreed to be its sponsor.

That center's director, Professor Michael Intriligator, cochaired our conference, "Ways to Help Resolve One of the World's Most Dangerous Conflicts." We invited scholars and other speakers

from India, Pakistan, Washington, D.C., and London to partici-
pate in the Sunday conference, which we hoped to conclude by
approving a set of appropriate resolutions to be sent to the United
Nations and to Washington, New Delhi, and London.

Our conference brought together some four hundred Kashmiri Muslims, Hindu Pandits, and other Indo-Pakistani scholars
and community leaders, filling our faculty center's largest room
and terrace, the first so diverse a group assembled to focus on the
Kashmir conflict on any campus in America. Many probing questions were asked during our morning sessions, stimulating fruitful
discussions of alternative paths to peace. But when London's Lord
Ahmed, the only Kashmiri Muslim in Britain's House of Lords,
started to speak on behalf of the Kashmiri community about the
conduct of Indian troops in Kashmir, who had "raped many Muslim women there," he ignited so volatile a response from Hindu
Indians in the room that most of them jumped to their feet,
shouting, "Lies! Retract! Throw him out!" Several of my own
colleagues screamed, "Boycott this meeting!" and advanced with
fists clenched toward the speaker. Our campus police, fearing a
riot, asked me to permit them to clear the room. My repeated
appeals for nonviolent civility and freedom of speech, however,
managed to convince most of our audience to return to their seats
a few minutes later; only a handful of angry Pandits stomped out,
urging all Indians to boycott the conference.

Somehow we managed to complete our conference without
further violent shouting or dire threats, and a few useful sugges-
tions did emerge by the end of that day on potential ways to resolve
the bitter Indo-Pakistani conflict over Kashmir. I had hoped that
we would draft a road map to peace that Sunday, but I felt grateful, when it had ended, that we had avoided bloodshed. I vividly

realized that if a few strong words spoken on our beautiful campus half a world away could trigger so much explosive anger and hatred, what terrifying damage daily gunfire and suicide bombings were doing in the once-happy Valley of Kashmir itself. I did not abandon all hope of helping to resolve that dreadful conflict, but I knew it would take far longer than I had once naïvely anticipated.

So many friends have helped me over the past four decades that I regret being unable to acknowledge my indebtedness to them all. I must first mention my Sanskrit guru, Professor W. Norman Brown, founding chair of the Department of South Asian Studies at the University of Pennsylvania, who awakened my interest in the tragic plight of Kashmir. Professors Holden Furber and Norman Palmer of Penn also shared with me their insights gained from many visits to Kashmir, as did Professor Richard Park of Berkeley and Vice-Chancellor J. Richard Sisson of UCLA. Many diplomat friends have added to my appreciation of how arduous their struggles have been in the pursuit of Indo-Pakistani peace, and I thank each of them for sharing their wisdom with me: Ambassador Robert B. Oakley, Ambassador Frank Wisner, Ambassador Jamsheed Marker, High Commissioner Kuldip Nayar, Ambassador Riaz Khokhar, Ambassador Teresita Schaffer, High Commissioner S. I. Abbas, Ambassador Abid Hussain, and Ambassador Rick Inderfurth.

I thank former Prime Minister Inder Kumar Gujral for his wise and abiding friendship over half a century and former Foreign Minister Raja Dinesh Singh, who also treated me as a member of his own family whenever I visited him in India, as his dear nephew, my former student Madhukar Shah, still does. Another of my dearest old Indian friends, Chhote Bharany, father of my former student Mahesh, has introduced me to more leading Indo-Pakistani negotiators for peace at his house parties than I have ever met in either Islamabad or New Delhi.

I am grateful to Pakistan's Foreign Minister Makhdoom S. M. Qureshi for his kind and warm encouragement at our recent meeting at Consul-General Abbas's house in Los Angeles. I must also thank my oldest Pakistani friends, Khalid Shamsul Hassan and Ardeshir Cowasjee, for teaching me so much about their troubled state. I thank Sardar Mumtaz Ali Bhutto and his son Ali for sharing his recent articles with me, and his daughter, Tasi, and her husband, Rizvan Kehar. Former Prime Minister and Minister of Finance Shaukat Aziz most kindly helped me during my past few visits to Pakistan.

Many wonderful friends in Los Angeles have introduced me to leaders of India and Pakistan, with whom I have been privileged to discuss Kashmir. My dearest Indian friend, Dr. A. S. Marwah, helped me meet with Prime Minister Manmohan Singh during my last visit to Delhi. And thanks to my ever-faithful friend Firoze Dordi, I have always been able to fly to India at short notice. Pakistan's good Dr. M. Shah and his brilliant wife, Fiza, founder of the finest female educational charity in Pakistan, Developments in Literacy, helped us to organize our Kashmir conference in 2002, as did Rafique Khan and his distinguished Kashmiri wife. Lloyd Cotson has long generously supported many academic projects at UCLA, least of which has been my quest for peace in South Asia, through our International Studies and Overseas Program when it was led by Dean John Hawkins, to whom I am also most grateful.

My best friend at UCLA, Harvey Perloff, founding dean of architecture and urban planning, taught me so much about problem-solving and futuristic planning that I can hardly thank him enough for his help whenever we talked about the problems of India, Pakistan, and Kashmir over lunch or dinner. Nor can I adequately thank his wife, Mimi, one of the greatest human beings I have ever had the privilege of knowing.

Stan Holwitz, my dear friend and great University of California Press editor, urged me to write this book long years ago, and when I finally finished my manuscript, he postponed his own retirement in order to help guide it through the Press's vetting process to publication, for which I most warmly thank him. Thanks as well to Laura Harger and Kalicia Pivirotto, both of whom have taken up Stan's unfinished editorial burdens.

Finally, as with every other creative effort of my now very long life, I thank my dearest Dorothy, to whom I proposed marriage fifty-seven short years ago, after which our wonderful sons, Daniel and Adam, were born, who with their brilliant and beautiful wives, Debra and Katy, have created our three remarkable grandchildren, Sam, Max, and Sabine, all of whom I most deeply love.

Introduction

More than six decades of freedom have quadrupled the population of India and transformed its democracy from the impoverished state of post–British India's Raj into the world's newest Asian superpower. India's military power and economy now approach those of the United States of America and China. The same six decades have diminished Pakistan from its promising origins as the world's largest Muslim state into an almost failed fragment of itself, more than half of its population having broken away to become independent Bangladesh in 1971. The only way in which India and Pakistan have remained virtually unchanged after sixty-three years is in their persistent conflict over the state of Jammu and Kashmir, the final tragic legacy of British India's 1947 partition, which followed the "shameful flight" of Great Britain's armed forces from India.[1] More than ten million terrified Hindus, Muslims, and Sikhs fled their ancestral homes that August, one million of whom died before reaching safe havens.

This book is the fruit of my own sixty years of preoccupation with India and Pakistan and their history. My first visit to India, in February 1948, brought me to Bombay on the day Mahatma Gandhi's ashes were immersed in the waters of Back Bay. I had never seen so many people: millions of silent mourners all dressed in white, waiting patiently from the dock's western Gateway to India to the crowded heart of that great city, surrounding the Taj Mahal Hotel, filling Victoria Station, Crawford Market, and Chaupati Beach, where a white ship bearing an urn with part of the Mahatma's ashes waited to sail out into the bay. I was shocked to learn that Gandhi, India's "little Father" (Bapu), had been assassinated by a Hindu Brahman who viewed the "Great Soul" (Mahatma) he murdered as a "Muslim-lover" determined to help Pakistan's army wrest Kashmir from India. It was my introduction to the complexity of multicultural India's society and the tragic consequences of partition's conflicts with neighboring Pakistan.

Fifty years later, in May 1998, India and Pakistan each successfully exploded five underground atomic bombs, joining the world's nuclear club. With their capitals and major cities less than ten ballistic missile–minutes from each other, the two countries have become the world's most dangerous match for the potential ignition of a nuclear war that could decimate South Asia and poison every region on earth. So unthinkable a global tragedy almost occurred in the summer of 1999 in Kargil and, once again, along the Kashmir Line of Control in 2002.

For over forty years I have been passionately concerned about the Indo-Pakistani conflict over Kashmir and the dreadful damage it has done to that beautiful state and its people. Since these two nations acquired nuclear arms, the dangers of their continued conflict have escalated disastrously. It is more urgent now than ever to resolve that dispute. Yet the possibility of nuclear war in South Asia has only increased in the past seven years, as Pakistan's polity lurched from unpopular martial rule under President General Musharraf to unstable civil rule under President Asif Ali Zardari. Pakistan's army is currently engaged in civil war with Taliban terrorists allied to Al-Qaeda (The Base) in Waziristan's North-West Frontier Province. Should even one of Pakistan's nuclear warheads fall into Taliban hands, it could be used by their suicide bombers to wreak havoc in India's largest city, as did the ten Pakistani terrorists who sailed from Karachi to Mumbai on November 26, 2008, launching three days and nights of atrocities there, killing 163 innocent people, setting fire to the Taj Mahal and Oberoi hotels, and desecrating the Chhatrapati Shivaji central railway terminus, Nariman House's Chabad Jewish Center, and the Cama Hospital. Trained and guided by Pakistan's Lashkar-e-Tayiba (Army of Allah), these terrorists were armed only with Kalashnikov rifles, hand grenades, and ordinary bombs, but the horror of that attack would have been magnified incalculably by a nuclear weapon. In July 2006, Lashkar trainers had launched suicide bombers against crowded commuter trains in Mumbai, killing 160 Indians during the morning rush hour.

Those tragic Mumbai attacks underscore the threat of the close proximity of two nuclear arsenals and the urgency to India and Pakistan of cooperating in their resolve to crush terrorism, whatever its national origins or religious beliefs. The two nations should quickly agree upon the creation of an efficient Indo-Pakistani anti-terror commission to prevent any future such attacks in cooperation with the United Nations, Interpol, and other intelligence agencies. Equally urgent, moreover, is the need to resolve the sixty-three-year-old Indo-Pakistani conflict over Kashmir, which has to date cost over 100,000 lives, mostly those of young Kashmiris, and countless billions of dollars in wasted resources, triggering three wars and almost igniting two nuclear confrontations in the past ten years that could have mushroomed to claim hundreds of millions of South Asian lives.

Some of the world's best minds have sought workable solutions to this complex problem, and many proposals and plans have been made to expedite the draft of a road map to peace on which India and Pakistan could finally agree. My guru of Indian civilization and Sanskrit, Dr. W. Norman Brown, founding chair of the Department of South Asian Regional Studies at the University of Pennsylvania, awakened my own awareness of this "most troublesome Kashmir conflict," as he called it, during my first year in his department, fifty-six years ago. Forty years later, my friend Professor John Kenneth Galbraith, President John F. Kennedy's ambassador to India, regretfully confessed that he'd "had no luck" in trying his best to persuade Prime Minister Nehru to agree to a UN–sponsored plebiscite for Kashmir. I had just begun to write my biography *Nehru: A Tryst with Destiny*, and I visited Galbraith before flying on to New Delhi, where I met with Nehru's sister "Nan," Madame Vijaya Lakshmi Pandit, and her daughter Rita Dhar, before flying into Kashmir.

Seeing how pervasively stifling a force India maintained in Srinagar, however, and how oppressive its presence was to so many of Kashmir's brightest young men and women, I then favored the UN Security Council's call for a plebiscite as perhaps the best and fairest self-determination solution. That remains Pakistan's preferred solution, but since 1954, it has been completely rejected by India. In light of the recently failed insurgency in

Kashmir, and Pakistan's nearly failed national status, it is no longer a viable option.

What, then, must be done to end this most prolonged, incredibly frustrating South Asian conflict before it explodes once again, endangering all the world with its toxic fallout? Before considering a potential solution to this problem, we must analyze its roots.

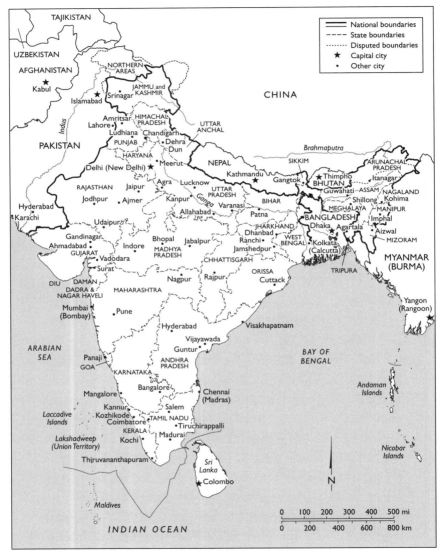

Map 1.   India.

ONE

The Historic Roots of the Problem

India and Pakistan were born to conflict generated by the partition of British India in August 1947. Britain's last viceroy, Admiral Lord Louis Mountbatten (known as "Dickie"), who had little understanding of India, foolishly halved the timetable allotted to him by British Prime Minister Clement Attlee's Labour cabinet to try to resolve the conflicts that divided India's political leaders and get them to agree to form a single federal dominion of independent India. Mahatma Gandhi and Jawaharlal Nehru, the leaders of the Indian National Congress party, had always wanted such a federal union. Since 1940, however, Muhammad Ali Jinnah and his Muslim League had demanded an independent Pakistan, whose Muslims would have their own government rather than remaining subordinate to India's Hindu majority. Mountbatten quickly grew bored listening to the repeated arguments of the two sides, and was so eager to put an end to hearing them squabble that he urged Attlee to advance Britain's withdrawal of its powers and troops to mid-August 1947 rather than waiting till the end of June 1948.

In less than ten weeks, a British lawyer, Cyril Radcliffe, who had never before set foot on Indian soil, presided over the partition of British India's two largest multicultural provinces, Punjab and Bengal. After first rushing Radcliffe to finish drawing the new maps in desperate haste, Mountbatten embargoed them as soon as Radcliffe was finished, refusing to allow even his own British governors of Punjab and Bengal to see where the new lines would be drawn, such that no troops could be stationed at key danger points along those incendiary provincial borders, no warnings could be posted for desperate people who, overnight, found themselves living in "enemy" countries rather than among relatives and friends. Fear and terror followed for millions, tsunamis of murder and looting drowning the Punjab's Sikhs, Hindus, and Muslims: trains filled with corpses steamed into Pakistan's Lahore and India's Amritsar stations as British troops filled every ship leaving the ports of Calcutta and Bombay, heading home to Cornwall and London even as Sir Cyril Radcliffe did, never looking back at the new border rivers of blood left behind.

Gandhi and Jinnah tried their best to slow Mountbatten down, pleading with him not to move so fast, knowing how terrified their people would be at what Mahatma Gandhi called the "vivisection of Mother India." But for Dickie, speed was always of the essence. Even Nehru, eager though he was to welcome the night of India's "tryst with destiny"[1] after a decade wasted in British prisons, begged Mountbatten not to rush the transfer of power, anticipating only too well the panic and dangers that would be unleashed by partition. But Mountbatten listened to no one. The Sikhs had asked him for a separate state, Sikhistan, with Amritsar as its capital, rightly fearing what Punjab's partition would do to them. And Bengalis had pleaded for a greater

Bangladesh, one with mighty Calcutta rather than tiny Dhaka as its capital, where all Bengali-speaking people, both Hindus and Muslims, could live together in peaceful harmony. But there was no time for them, either, on Mountbatten's large office calendar, each day of which he swiftly ripped off first thing every morning. So the juggernaut rolled on, crushing a million innocents under its giant wheels that fateful fall.

At that time, three-quarters of British India's some 400 million people were Hindus, most of the remaining quarter being Muslims, plus six million Sikhs and a million or so Parsis, Christians, and Jews. Hinduism's ancient roots are buried in the fecund soil of India's river valleys, primarily the Indus, where archaeological artifacts over four thousand years old have been unearthed. Symbols of mother-goddess worship as well as yogic practices associated with Lord Shiva in his iconic phallic form have been found in major centers of ancient Indus civilization, especially at Mohenjo-daro in Sind and Harappa in Punjab. A complex hierarchy of social castes is also reflected in the urban divisions of those remarkable Indus cities, whose arts and technological sophistication bear many other distinctive traces of contemporary Indian civilization. Long before the birth of Christianity, Hinduism's *Rig Veda* preserved Sanskrit hymns addressed to the thirty-three gods of its pantheon, and Hindu philosophy developed six remarkable systems of logical reasoning and abstract thought, including transcendental Vedanta philosophy, that continue to dazzle and fascinate students both in India and throughout the Western world.

The epic poems of ancient India, the *Mahabharata* and *Ramayana*, are still revered throughout India as the *Iliad* and *Odyssey* are in the West. Vishnu, the great solar divinity of Hinduism, has many earthly emanations *(avataras)*, the most popular among which are Rama, Krishna, and the Buddha. Near the dawn of the Christian era, Hindus began to build beautiful temples, each dedicated to one or many of their gods, loving figures of which were usually carved in stone on one or more of those temples' façades.

Islam was born in Saudi Arabia in 622 C.E. and was first brought to South Asia by Arab warriors in 711 C.E. Starting in the eleventh century, Afghan, Persian, and Central Asian Muslim armies invaded India over its rugged North-West Frontier passes, destroying Hindu temples, whose images were anathema to Islam's iconoclastic devotees. Through the sixteenth century, those Muslim invaders continued to hammer away at Hindu temple cities, looting them and taking hostages back over the passes to Afghanistan. After 1206 C.E., when the Delhi sultanate was born, Muslim Afghan kings settled down to rule in North India's more salubrious clime, even as Central Asia's Great Mughal *padishahs* (emperors) would, following Babur's conquest of Delhi in 1526 C.E.

Hindus were initially forced to "surrender" *(Islam)* or face death. Mahmud of Ghazni, first of the invading Afghans, was known as "The Sword of Islam." But it soon became clear to Muslim monarchs that they could not hope to govern so vast and complex a world as India without local allies to collect their taxes and establish administrative systems that worked. So they granted Hindus the tolerant dispensation earlier offered by the Prophet Muhammad to Christians and Jews as "Peoples of the Book," allowing them to pay a "head tax" *(jizya)* to remain Hindus. Brahmans and other high-caste Hindus readily accepted that option, though they resented being obliged to pay for the privilege of continuing to worship their own gods in their own country. Millions of lower-caste and outcaste (Untouchable) Hindus preferred to convert to Islam, however, since they had no money and soon were attracted by the better-paid work available to them as Muslim converts. Others were lured to convert by the saintly Sufi mystics of Kashmir and Bengal, whose poetry and gentle teachings of God's love and compassionate grace for all humans won their hearts. Islam's universal democratic ethic also appealed to outcaste Hindus sick of Brahmanic domination. Nor was it difficult for them to "become" Muslim, which required them merely to affirm Islam's credo: "There is no God but Allah, and Muhammad is the Prophet of God," in Arabic. Brighter converts would also soon learn to pray five times daily, facing toward Mecca, to abstain from pork and wine, and to try their best to follow the "path to the watering place" trod by the Prophet.

By 1858, when Great Britain established its imperial Raj over most of India, about one-quarter of South Asia's population was Muslim, primarily the progeny of Hindu converts. Before that century ended, India's brightest young Hindus and modernist Muslims had brilliantly mastered Western education in English. Inspired by Milton, Bentham, Macaulay, Mill, and Morley, they demanded liberalism's freedoms and utilitarian reforms for India, citing the repeated promises of reform made by Empress Victoria, Britain's Prime Minister William Gladstone, and the enlightened British viceroy Lord Ripon. Following the lead of the civil servant–ornithologist Allan Octavian Hume, who inspired the creation of the Indian National Congress in 1885, Gopal Krishna Gokhale, Mahatma Gandhi's political guru, became Liberal Secretary of State John Morley's leading Indian adviser on reforms in 1906. Gokhale could have become the first Indian viceroy had it not been for a split in the Indian National Congress, which was triggered by the orthodox Brahman Bal Gangadhar Tilak's feud with Gokhale and his liberal friends. Tilak launched a revolutionary "New Party" that broke away from the moderate anglophile Congress in 1907.[2] The brilliant Muslim lawyer M. A. Jinnah, whose ambition at this time was to become the Muslim Gokhale, was drawn to the Congress by its enlightened leadership. Later, he joined the more conservative Muslim League as well. Jinnah drafted a joint platform, adopted by both the Congress and the League, for post–World War I constitutional reforms, which was presented to the viceroy of British India and the secretary of state for India in 1916.[3] Had that "Lucknow Pact," as the earliest Congress-League proposal for Dominion status for India was called, been accepted by competing Indian factions, and implemented by Great Britain's government after World War I, all of the subsequent agonies of partition could have been avoided.

But Britain's pre–World War I Liberal era ended without such enlightened reforms. Waves of harsh Tory repression returned to shatter Congress's dreams of freedom's reward for their loyal wartime cooperation in support of the Raj. Muslims were also bitterly disappointed when the secret Sykes-Picot wartime agreements, made by by the victorious Anglo-French allies to despoil the Ottoman Empire, came to light. The popular pan-Islamic Khilafat Movement was most strongly supported by Mahatma Gandhi as the first plank of his postwar Satyagraha (Hold Fast to the Truth) noncooperation movement against British duplicity and tyranny in 1919. That movement collapsed, however, when Mustafa Kemal Atatürk, the first president of the Turkish Republic, abolished the Caliphate. Gandhi meanwhile had turned to more revolutionary action against the Raj, calling upon his followers in 1920 to launch a multiple boycott of all things British, including law courts, titles, and Western education. British imports of every variety, especially cotton clothing and silk dresses, were burned in huge open-air fires, redolent of ancient Vedic sacrifices. Jinnah opposed such mass protests, fearing that they would provoke violence, despite Gandhi's insistence that nonviolence *(a-himsa)* must be central to his movement, considering it no less than God, even as he valued truth *(satya)*, the ancient *Rig Veda*'s term for the real.

Jinnah's objections were ignored by Gandhi's Indian National Congress, however, and he was shouted down by its vast majority, who considered him a Muslim tool of the British and drove him out of its meeting, and out of politics entirely. He rented law offices in London, pleading appeals before the Privy Council, living in a splendid house in Hampstead near the Heath, until several of his closest Bombay Muslim friends invited him to lead their moribund Muslim League, which Jinnah quickly revitalized, becoming its permanent president. Mahatma Gandhi and Motilal Nehru then led the Congress party.

In 1930, Motilal's only son, Jawaharlal, presided over the first of his many annual Congress sessions, drafting its passionate demand for complete freedom *(purna swaraj)* from British rule. The radical, charismatic Nehru led the Congress party to victory in every electoral campaign he undertook. He was not only Gandhi's political heir, but also the darling of India's intellectuals. Men and women alike were drawn to join the Congress thanks to his idealism and personal magnetism. Ardent socialist that he was, Nehru considered Jinnah a reactionary reflection of the outmoded English liberalism of the previous century, and never took him or his League seriously as a challenge to Congress dominance. When Congress won the majority in most provinces of British India in nationwide elections of 1937 and Jinnah called for coalition Congress-League cabinets in the largest multicultural provinces of North India, Nehru replied that only "two parties" remained in India, "Congress and the British." Jinnah responded: "There is a *third* party—the Muslims!"

Jinnah devoted the last decade of his life, and that of British India, to proving that his League commanded the support of the majority of India's Muslim population, whom he claimed wanted their own separate nation-state of Pakistan (Land of the Pure), also an acrostic of Punjab, Afghania (the North-West Frontier), Kashmir, Sind, and Baluchistan. In March 1940, when the League's Pakistan resolution was unanimously carried at its annual session in Lahore, Jinnah was hailed as its *Quaid-i-Azam* (Great Leader). He devoted the rest of his life to convincing the British, as well as every South Asian Muslim, of the validity of his demand. Few took him seriously at first. Most Congress leaders considered him mad, but, during World War II, when Gandhi and Nehru rejected the British viceroy's appeals for Congress support against the Axis, Jinnah and his League supported the Raj, as did all the Muslim troops of Punjab. Winston Churchill and the wartime viceroys Linlithgow and Wavell considered Jinnah Britain's best friend, while they viewed Gandhi, Nehru, Patel, and other Congress leaders as traitors to be locked up behind bars till the war's end.

Britain's postwar fatigue and a growing sterling balance indebtedness to India for shipments of Punjabi wheat and other vital wartime supplies, which kept British as well as Indian troops alive on the Western Front and in North Africa, left Attlee's new Labour government as sick and tired of Congress-League squabbling as Churchill's wartime cabinet had been. Even the radical Stafford Cripps, Congress's best friend in the cabinet, grew frustrated with Gandhi and Nehru as they carped and bickered over Britain's last constitutional offer, which Cripps had drafted for the 1946 cabinet mission that Labour's elderly secretary of state for India and Burma, Lord Frederick Pethick-Lawrence, led. Jinnah accepted that federal plan, which would have given him most of what he wanted, but without calling it Pakistan. Nehru then balked, however, and Gandhi raised more questions, which finally drove the weary Cripps to abandon India in anger and disgust. His three-tier plan would have loosely united virtually autonomous groups of provinces of what are now India, Pakistan, and Bangladesh under a weak central umbrella controlling foreign affairs, defense, and currency, also resolving religious arguments among those three multiprovincial state groups. Had it only been given a chance, that complex but wise plan might have saved South Asia the agonies of three wars and the incalculable cost of partition.

But when Cripps came home admitting defeat, there seemed little more that Attlee could do. So, as Mountbatten's friend Noël Coward put it, "The position having become impossible, they call on Dickie!" Mountbatten took up the last viceroy's job as lightheartedly as he did most things, with royal panache, informing "Cousin Bertie," King George, that he viewed the idea of breaking India's political deadlock as challenging as a game of polo: "The last Chukka in India—12 goals down."[4] He got so bored, however, trying to bring Nehru, Gandhi, and Jinnah to agree upon a single plan that he swiftly opted for partition as the simplest solution.

Cyril Radcliffe was invited to India to chair the Punjab and Bengal Partition Commissions, each with two constantly divided Congress and League lawyers on it, leaving Radcliffe himself to finish drawing the two new dominions' boundary lines on the sorely inadequate maps he'd been given. The commissions had been appointed merely to divide both provinces along "Muslim versus non-Muslim majority Districts," yet Radcliffe's Punjab line cut through the heart of Punjab's central canal colony land, where some six million Sikhs lived, since Mountbatten refused to consider Sikh demands for a state of their own. Nor could Radcliffe resist pressure from Mountbatten, who had accepted Nehru's flattering invitation to serve as independent India's first governor-general, and so acceded to Nehru's passionate insistence that the Gurdaspur District of Punjab be awarded to India, despite its Muslim majority, since without it, India would have been deprived of direct road access to the Vale of Kashmir. Nehru also demanded that the Muslim-majority subdistrict of Ferozepur, with its mighty hydroelectric generators, be included in India's Punjab for vital strategic reasons. Mountbatten, judging the strategic risk of losing Ferozepur too high a price for India to pay, persuaded Radcliffe to redraw his initial Punjab line accordingly, though neither he nor Mountbatten ever admitted the latter's "pressure."[5]

Anguished Hindu-Sikh refugee columns grew into human flood lines as they left the burning city of Lahore, trudging twenty miles east to the border town at Wagah, and another twenty miles beyond that to Indian Punjab's new capital, Amritsar, sacred to all Sikhs. The founder of Sikhism, Guru Nanak, was born in West Punjab's Sheikhupura District; his Gurdwara temple, marking that sacred birthplace, Nankana Sahib, was left to Pakistan and remained a place of pilgrimage for Indian Sikhs. The saintly Guru Nanak won converts wherever he went, and his gentle message of tolerance, charity, and hard work, taught in his "true words," are preserved as scripture in the *Guru Granth Sahib* of the Sikhs, worshiped in Amritsar's Golden Temple. Mughal emperors brutally murdered two of Sikhism's ten Gurus, who refused to convert to Islam, and Guru Govind Singh, the tenth and last Guru, launched a war to the death against Mughal tyranny, renaming his Sikh (Student) disciples Singhs (Lions), welding them into a mighty Khalsa (Army of the Pure) of fearless sword-wielding warriors pledged in bonds of blood to destroy the Mughal tyrants. The British subsequently recruited Sikhs into their Indian army, and their fighting prowess and spirit continue to be represented in India's armed forces, as well as by national leaders like the current prime minister, Dr. Manmohan Singh. Sikhism today has become a global faith, though most Sikhs still live in India, and all try to visit Amritsar at least once a year.

Partition's bitter "wooden loaf," as Gandhi called it, thus poisoned the taste of freedom for Congress's leaders, all of whom had so eagerly awaited independence. Nehru sorely questioned his own judgment in accepting the partition scheme that Mountbatten had pushed upon him, urging him not to hesitate. "And yet, the consequences of that partition have been so terrible that one is inclined to think that anything else would have been preferable," Nehru sadly reflected after it was too late.[6] The legacy of hatred left by the tragedy of partition induced the leaders of both new dominions to mistrust each other, seek vengeance, and believe the worst of each other's motives. Two months after winning their precious freedom, India and Pakistan embarked on their first war, over the former state of Jammu and Kashmir.

TWO

The First Indo-Pakistani War

The earliest written history of South Asia, Kashmir's ancient *Rājataranginī* (River of Kings), dating back to 1148 C.E., records both the wisdom of Kashmir's greatest rulers and the cruelty of its most violent.[1] Its first author, Kalhana, commences by bowing to the Hindu Lord Shiva, whose many consorts include the mother goddess Parvati, one of whose terrestrial names was Kashmira. India's great Buddhist emperor Aśoka, who reigned over Mauryan India from 269 to 232 B.C.E., founded Kashmir's capital of Srinagar on the banks of the river Vitasta during his brief visit to that peaceful valley. The lovely city, which soon embraced Dal Lake and later came to be called the Venice of India, lured to its garden-filled precincts people of every faith: Hindu, Muslim, Buddhist, and Christian. Their craftsmanship and artistry blended to create a uniquely tolerant, beautifully harmonious eclectic culture called Kashmiryat, a microcosmic reflection of South Asia's complexity.

Kanishka, the greatest Central Asian Kushana monarch who conquered North India, whose reign spanned two decades around

100 C.E., hosted a Buddhist council at a monastery near Srinagar. He invited to Kashmir Chinese as well as Indian monks, who are said to have recorded all 300,000 stanzas of Mahayana Buddhism's *Tripitaka* canon on copper plates, which unfortunately have since been lost. Kashmir's northwestern region, Ladakh, with its capital of Leh, has since Kanishka's reign remained Buddhist.

During the eighth century, Kashmir expanded into Tibet under the "Alexander" of Kashmiri history, the Hindu warrior-king Lalitaditya, whose appetite for conquest added as much to his kingdom's prosperity as to its territory. Lalitaditya, Kashmir's most powerful Hindu monarch, was tolerant of his Buddhist as well as his Hindu subjects, supporting scholars of both faiths and funding the construction of many temples and monasteries.

Islam first entered Kashmir in the sixth annual attack into India by the Afghan sultan Mahmud of Ghazni, early in the eleventh century. But Mahmud was forced to turn back by winter weather and reached only the outskirts of Srinagar. A series of feuding Hindu monarchs subsequently stripped Kashmir of much of its domain; Ladakh and Jammu broke off to become independent kingdoms by the dawn of the thirteenth century. Sufi saints then wandered into the valley, converting many Hindu peasants with their message of love. In the early part of the next century, Rinchin, a prince of Ladakh, forced to flee from Tibet, came to Kashmir with many followers and his Hindu queen, Kota Rani. She outlived her husband, was famed for her beauty and independence, and was admired throughout Kashmir as its greatest female ruler. (The most famous modern Kashmiri woman to rule all of India, however, was Jawaharlal Nehru's talented daughter Indira Gandhi.)

Many Muslim sultans of Shams-ud-din's dynasty ruled over Kashmir for 222 years, with none greater than Zain-ud-Abidin (1420–70). His genius was never to forget that Kashmiri Hindus and Buddhists were equally loyal and, if treated with toleration, would prove as helpful to his land's growth and its arts as the brilliant Sufi saints and poets of his court. His patronage of drama revived its practice throughout Kashmir, just as his generous support of local rug-makers, shawl-weavers, wood-carvers, and papier-mâché artists brought all those Kashmiri crafts to their peaks of artistic perfection, hailed the world over. Hindu pandits wrote of the Vale of Kashmir becoming a smiling garden of industry in Zain's reign.

Akbar, the "Great" Mughal, annexed Kashmir to his imperium in 1586. Akbar's son Jahangir (1606–27) loved to breathe the fragrant air of Kashmir, which he often visited with his Persian consort, Nur Mahal (Light of the World), planting their royal gardens of Shalimar and Nishat in the environs of Dal Lake. This happy valley then became, indeed, the "paradise on Earth," about which Ireland's national bard Thomas Moore was inspired to pen his popular poem *Lalla Rookh*, celebrating its beauty and attracting generations of European tourists there.

The decline and fall of the Mughal Empire in the latter part of the eighteenth century left Kashmir ripe for conquest by the Pathan plunderer Ahmad Shah Abdali, later named Durrani. Afghan invaders brought such pain and penury to Kashmir's gentle people that some of them went to Punjab to appeal to its Sikh Maharaja Ranjit Singh to come to Srinagar to save them. But one-eyed Ranjit proved little better than his Muslim precursors in dealing with Kashmir's population. He was, however, strong and shrewd enough to keep the British Company Raj at bay.

But, after his death in 1839, Dogra Rajput Gulab Singh turned against the Sikhs he had earlier served and helped British troops seize control of the valley.

Gulab Singh later bought Kashmir from the British for a nominal sum, and, having earlier received Jammu from Ranjit Singh, he combined them into the largest of British India's six hundred princely states, Jammu and Kashmir, which in 1846 the British turned over to Gulab Singh and his male heirs in perpetuity. Gulab's son, Ranbir Singh, proved as helpful to his British overlords as his father had been, sending Kashmiri troops and guns to Delhi in 1858 to oust Bengal's Sepoy mutineers from that Mughal capital. Ranbir was given Britain's full twenty-one-gun salute status at the top of India's princely pecking order. Devout Hindu that he was, he funded the building of many new temples in Jammu, employing all of his Dogra relatives and Kashmir's Hindu pandits but leaving his Muslim subjects impoverished and dissatisfied. After Ranbir died in 1885, his son Pratap Singh inherited Kashmir, which he ruled till his own death in 1925. He died without heir but was succeeded by his nephew Hari Singh, who most enjoyed visiting London, where he soon learned of the attractions of Soho and Kensington, focusing more time and attention on women than on the plight of his poor Kashmiri people. Mountbatten had early befriended Hari Singh, and helped keep his name out of London's tabloid press in a notorious scandal where he was known only as "Mr. A."

In mid-August 1947, Viceroy Lord Mountbatten had no hesitation about leaving the destiny of Kashmir's four million subjects, 77 percent of whom were Muslims, to the personal choice of Maharaja Hari Singh. Only Hari could not make up his mind, fearing the socialist Nehru's India almost as much as he did the prospect of joining Jinnah's Pakistan. He hoped instead to keep Jammu and Kashmir independent, the Switzerland of Asia. That dream was never accepted as feasible by either India or Pakistan. Kashmir's beauty, strategic value, and ethnic complexity may resemble Switzerland's, but neither of its powerful neighbors was willing to indulge Hari Singh's fantasy or to wait very long for him to decide which dominion to join.

By October 1947, two months after Britain withdrew its forces, Muslim peasants of Poonch refused to pay their land taxes to Hindu landlords, whose guards opened fire. The Muslims fled to Pakistan, where tribal frontier Pathans were inflamed by their reports and volunteered to help them liberate Kashmir from Hindu control. British officers who had opted to remain in Pakistan packed thousands of such Pathans into trucks that headed down Baramulla Road into Kashmir. They quickly seized Muzaffarabad, the subsequent capital of Pakistan's Azad (Free) Kashmir.

India's government in New Delhi responded swiftly to this invasion of Prime Minister Pandit Nehru's "home" state of Kashmir. Though Nehru's great-grandfather had left Kashmir to move with his family to Delhi, Nehru always considered Kashmir his ancestral home, and he ordered India's First Sikh Battalion flown up to Srinagar to defend it less than forty-eight hours after news of the Pakistani invasion reached Delhi. India's troops secured the airport and drove the undisciplined Pathans back to Muzaffarabad. Jinnah then tried to send two of Pakistan's regular divisions into the battle, but was blocked by Field Marshal Claude Auchinleck, supreme commander of British Commonwealth troops of both dominions, who flew to Pakistan to warn Jinnah that unless he withdrew his order, he would have to order every

British officer in Pakistan's army to "stand down." Since Pakistan at that time relied much more heavily than India on British officers, commanded by General Sir Douglas Gracey, Jinnah was forced to relent. Pakistani volunteer soldiers in mufti were sent in, but proved an insufficient force to drive out the Indian army.

In mid-December 1947, Nehru told his cabinet that "what is happening in Kashmir State is not merely a frontier raid but a regular war." On 3 January 1948, then, India brought charges of Pakistan's aggression to the UN Security Council, calling upon it to "take immediate and effective action" to stop Pakistan.[2] The ensuing Security Council debate over Kashmir became one of its longest and most bitterly argued marathons. Pakistan's first foreign minister, Muhammad Zafrullah Khan, opened the debate by insisting that the conflict in Kashmir was merely an extension internationally of British India's Hindu-Muslim communal conflicts of the past century. The only appropriate way, he insisted, of resolving the conflict was to ascertain the will of Kashmir's population by taking an impartial plebiscite in that state, to be administered by UN representatives.

India's UN ambassador, Gopalaswamy Ayyangar, articulated Nehru's charge that Pakistan had launched an illegal invasion of Kashmir, insisting that India would agree to a plebiscite only after Pakistan had completely vacated its aggression, withdrawing all its troops and tribal invaders from the state. Pakistan replied it would withdraw its protection of Muslims in the portion of Kashmir it controlled only after India withdrew its entire army from Srinagar and the rest of the Vale of Kashmir. Spokesmen for both countries repeated those positions every time the council met to consider the subject. By the end of January 1948, the Security

Council decided to appoint a UN Commission on India and Pakistan (UNCIP), which was to visit South Asia as early as possible to investigate the facts and difficulties on the ground.

On 21 April 1948, the Security Council resolved to send its commission to New Delhi and Karachi to help restore peace and order to Kashmir by preparing the ground there for a plebiscite. The council also called for a cease-fire in Kashmir, to begin on 1 January 1949. A plebiscite administrator was to be nominated by the UN secretary-general, formally appointed by the government of Jammu and Kashmir to ensure the freedom and impartiality of the election.

U.S. Admiral Chester W. Nimitz was the first plebiscite administrator to be nominated, but India judged him unacceptable. A UN cease-fire line in Kashmir, to be monitored by UN observers, was demarcated in July 1949. At year's end, Canada's Security Council president, General A. G. L. McNaughton, attempted to mediate an agreement himself, but failed. "No plebiscite is possible in Kashmir before the refugees are rehabilitated," Nehru insisted. "The price of freedom and progress is blood, sweat and tears." In Srinagar, Nehru told his growing army, "The Kashmir operation is a fight for the freedom of India."

On 14 March 1950, the Security Council passed a resolution calling upon India and Pakistan to prepare themselves for a Kashmir plebiscite within five months. Australia's Sir Owen Dixon was appointed plebiscite mediator; he stayed a month in Kashmir, then shuttled between New Delhi and Karachi until 22 August 1950, when he gave up trying to get the two sides to agree to any formula. Sir Owen's impartiality as a jurist-mediator convinced him that the best solution to the Kashmir conflict would be to partition the state between its Muslim-majority Vale of Kashmir, most of whose inhabitants seemed to favor Pakistan, and its Hindu-Buddhist majorities in Jammu and Ladakh, who apparently favored India. Nehru rejected the idea of partition, however, and refused ever to consider turning over the Vale of Kashmir to Pakistan. India's Hindu High Commissioner to Pakistan, Sri Prakasha, once had the temerity to suggest to Mountbatten that the "wisest" thing India could do in Kashmir was to "let Pakistan have it," but Nehru angrily vetoed that proposal.

In March 1951, the Security Council adopted a new resolution on Jammu and Kashmir, and Dr. Frank Graham, former North Carolina senator and later president of the University of North Carolina, flew to South Asia as the last nominee sent out to administer a UN plebiscite there. Graham found Nehru unresponsive to his numerous appeals and proposals. That July, Prime Minister Liaquat Ali Khan of Pakistan informed British Commonwealth colleagues that heavy fire had been exchanged across the Kashmir cease-fire line, along which nine-tenths of India's army was deployed. India countered by charging Pakistan with sending armed terrorists over the line and encouraging them to wage jihad. After both countries brought up more troops and moved heavy artillery closer to the line, Liaquat agreed to meet with Nehru in New Delhi to seek some formula to settle their dispute over Kashmir. Shortly before the date scheduled for their New Delhi summit meeting, however, Liaquat was assassinated at Pakistan's army headquarters in Rawalpindi on 16 October 1951. He had just begun to address his officer corps, urging patience in dealing with India, when shots silenced him. Liaquat's Afghan assassin was instantly shot dead by an officer inside that stadium. No investigation ever led to punishment of the killers who had conspired to murder Pakistan's first prime minister.

Since Liaquat's assassination, Pakistan's army has remained the most powerful institution of Pakistan's polity. "Most nations have an army," Nehru once said, "but Pakistan's army has a nation." Jinnah's popular Muslim League Party had initially trained a cadre of civil administrators to run Pakistan. However, after Pakistan's army emerged from the command of British colonels and generals, it swiftly usurped power from Pakistan's political leaders and civil bureaucrats. Punjabi and Pathan generals have since 1951 ruled virtually unchallenged from their headquarters in Rawalpindi. Pakistan's generals have always believed that India was merely playing for time by agreeing to hold a plebiscite. They felt certain that Nehru would never surrender Kashmir, no matter how large a majority of its Muslims might vote for Pakistan. Liaquat was considered too weak to fight for Kashmir's Muslims, as Jinnah had so forcefully done. Nor did the army have any faith in East Pakistan's Bengali politicians, who cared little about distant Kashmir. India soon insisted that Kashmir's Constituent Assembly, elected in 1953, was nothing less than a truly representative body chosen by plebiscite, the clear voice of Kashmir's people. Kashmir's most popular leader, Sheikh Muhammad Abdullah, had been supported by Nehru against Maharaja Hari Singh. In 1953, however, when Abdullah favored a UN plebiscite, Nehru felt it was time to arrest him, and he kept Kashmir's Muslim "Lion" behind Indian bars for more than a decade.

By 1954, the Cold War played a role in exacerbating the Indo-Pakistani conflict over Kashmir.[3] Pakistan—which joined the United States and Great Britain in the Central Treaty Organization (CENTO) and the Southeast Asia Treaty Organization (SEATO), military alliances designed to contain Soviet expansion—received substantial military support. India, which was much closer to the Soviet Union thanks to Nehru's socialism and early visit to Moscow, refused to join any of Washington's Cold War alliances. President Eisenhower assured Nehru that no U.S. aid to Pakistan would ever be used against India, but Nehru felt he knew better, and, to counter similar shipments to Karachi from Washington, India turned to the Soviet Union for planes, tanks, and artillery.

On India's Republic Day, 26 January 1957, Kashmir's Constituent Assembly adopted its own state constitution, proclaiming Jammu and Kashmir an integral part of India. A quarter of the hundred seats in the Legislative Assembly in Srinagar were left empty, reserved for future members to be elected from the Pakistani-occupied portion of Kashmir. They have never been filled, and India has insisted that since every election in Jammu and Kashmir has been a true reflection of the free will of its people, no external plebiscite supervised by UNCIP need ever be considered.

Map 2. Kashmir.

THREE

The Second Indo-Pakistani War

The UN cease-fire line in Kashmir could not prevent heavy artillery from firing over it or Pakistani infiltrators from crossing it. Nor were there ever enough UN monitors to do more than report violations of the cease-fire they were employed to enforce. The United Nations had no army of its own, after all, nor money enough to keep more than a few monitors posted at distant stations along that porous line.

Pakistan's chief of army staff in 1957, General Muhammad Ayub Khan, was furious when India announced that the adoption of Jammu and Kashmir's new constitution made that state an integral part of the Indian Union. Colonel Ayub, a graduate of Britain's Royal Military College at Sandhurst, had been in command of Punjab's small partition-border force, which he kept in barracks in 1947, failing to stop any of the murders of Hindus and Sikhs fleeing Lahore. After Pakistan joined SEATO, Ayub flew to Georgia in the United States for special forces training, and also visited Texas and Langley, Virginia, headquarters of the CIA, returning to Pakistan as its top general. Ayub was a good soldier, but during his sojourn in the United States he had acquired political ambitions, and upon returning home he soon lost patience with what he called the "idiocy" of Pakistan's civil leaders and consensus-seeking politicians. Ayub had no trouble convincing President General Iskandar Mirza, a Parsi, of his views about the ineptitude of Pakistan's politicians, especially voluble Bengalis like Prime Minister H. S. Suhrawardy, whose tenure had lasted only a year when he was forced to resign by a vote of no confidence in October 1957. A year later, Mirza abrogated Pakistan's constitution and appointed Ayub Khan chief martial law administrator.

That was Pakistan's first military coup. Elections scheduled to have been held a few months after it started were canceled because of "lack of decorum, and the prostitution of Islam for political ends," as Ayub later put it.[1] The coup was bloodless. New American tanks appeared ominously at major intersections of every large Pakistani city that October morning in 1958, and traffic and trains were kept moving.

Twenty days after the coup, President Mirza was forced to resign and left Pakistan with his family, flying off to London exile. Ayub Khan awarded himself the title of president, establishing a pattern followed by all three of Pakistan's subsequent coup leaders. Explaining that it was the army's responsibility to protect Pakistan's people, since its politicians were letting the country "go to the dogs," Ayub said that he took up his new burden in a spirit of "selfless sacrifice." He dismissed as false charges that he coveted political power and insisted that he planned to return to barracks just as soon as order was restored. But that would take a decade longer.

Ayub hoped to reach some agreement with Nehru on Kashmir, and proposed to fly to India himself, but Nehru rejected the offer, viewing Ayub as a mere "lackey" of Washington, as well as the usurper of Pakistani civil power. After that, Ayub left the issue of Kashmir in the hands of his young foreign minister, Zulfikar Ali Bhutto, who engaged India's foreign minister, Swaran Singh, in six months of futile talks, seeking in vain to resolve their dispute over Kashmir.[2] Zulfi also convinced Ayub of the importance of courting China, whose charismatic foreign minister, Chou En-lai, most effectively challenged Nehru's claims to India's leadership of the uncommitted Third World of Asia and Africa. Sino-Pakistani friendship has been a keystone of Pakistan's foreign policy from 1962 to the present thanks to Bhutto. Two months before his first meeting with Swaran Singh in December 1962, China had invaded India over its northern border, wiping out Indian troops there and advancing virtually unopposed toward Assam's capital, Gauhati. This defeat of Indian forces cost Nehru's cabinet colleague V.K. Krishna Menon his job as minister of defense. Bhutto consolidated his diplomatic friendship with China by reaching agreement with Chou on Pakistan's northern border, ceding some 2,000 square miles of Kashmir State to China. Outraged, India vehemently protested to the UN Security Council that this unilateral action was unlawful, and Nehru almost aborted the Indo-Pakistani talks before they were launched. Nothing more came of that diplomatic marathon, however, than an agreement to stop engaging in "adverse propaganda."[3]

Ayub focused his own energy on introducing a constitution to Pakistan based on what he called "basic democracy." The vast majority of an electorate of sixty thousand "basic democrats," most of them young men from military families, and each representing a district of Pakistan, voted to express complete confidence in Ayub Khan when he held a single-question referendum on his worthiness to serve as president. Ayub and his enterprising son worked hard at creating a beautiful new capital for Pakistan, Islamabad, built mostly of white marble and stone on the virgin land of Punjab's Potwar Plateau, north of Rawalpindi. Before the end of 1964, crowded Karachi's old federal offices and embassies were abandoned and their occupants moved to Islamabad's handsome new buildings.

Early in 1965, Ayub received his first shipment of new U.S. M48 tanks, with their 90 mm guns. Foreign Minister Bhutto urged Ayub to promote himself to field marshal, since there were by then so many generals in Pakistan's army. Bhutto also proposed the liberation of Kashmir, explaining that Nehru's death in 1964 would make it easy for Pakistan to "take back" that state. Nehru's successor, tiny Lal Bahadur Shastri, Bhutto believed, was no match for the giant Ayub, who would initially test Shastri's resolve in the desolate salt marsh Rann of Kutch, the southern portion of West Pakistan's border with India, which remained dry till annual monsoon rains started to flood it in June.

That April, Pakistani patrols opened fire on several Indian border guards at Sardar in the Rann, triggering responding fire, soon after which a swift column of Patton tanks rumbled with ease through lightly defended Indian barricades. Ayub's new tanks performed so well, indeed, that he was eager to test them again, in Kashmir. Bhutto assured Ayub that he had firm intelligence indicating very strong support throughout the Vale of Kashmir for a Pakistani invasion. Early in August 1965, UN observers reported heavy artillery fire from Pakistan over the cease-fire line, followed by major infiltration. Bhutto boldly denied any Pakistani incitement, however, insisting to the press in mid-August that Kashmir was experiencing a "spontaneous uprising against Indian tyranny."

However, Prime Minister Shastri, speaking from the top of Delhi's Red Fort, charged Pakistan with having invaded Kashmir, and vowed to his nation that such aggression against India would never be allowed to succeed. Before the end of August, Indian and Pakistani regular units were engaged along the former cease-fire line. Pakistan's "Operation Gibraltar," launched late in July at Bhutto's urgent insistence, proved a disaster. Most of Pakistan's infiltrators over the high-altitude line froze to death before Ayub's "Operation Grand Slam" could deliver its knockout blow against Jammu from Sialkot, hoping to capture Akhnur and thus cut the only rail link from India to Kashmir. India's strategic planners were much wiser than Ayub and Bhutto, opening the floodgates of their nearest dams and trapping Pakistan's tank corps in deep mud, then launching a three-pronged attack across the Indo-Pakistani international border in Punjab, aimed at the defenseless capital of Lahore. Bhutto had assured Ayub that this could never happen, saying he was positive that Shastri would never dare to attack Lahore. Now Ayub was faced with the most humiliating defeat of his life as India's tanks rolled into sight of his greatest city's Mughal Fort and Shalimar Gardens. It was his worst nightmare come true, and, in desperation, he phoned U.S. President Lyndon Johnson, begging him to arrange an immediate cease-fire with India.

Johnson froze all U.S. shipments of arms and ammunition to South Asia, and then spoke with Russia's Premier Alexei Kosygin, who invited Ayub and Shastri to Tashkent in Central Asia for a peace conference.

They met on 4 January 1966, and India's shortest leader and Pakistan's tallest, South Asia's David and Goliath, soon learned to like and respect each other. "Instead of fighting each other, let us start fighting poverty, disease and ignorance,"[4] Shastri urged Ayub that first day, and Ayub nodded agreement. Bhutto, who was there at Ayub's side, frowned and sank lower in his seat, angrily sulking as he watched Ayub respond with warm approval to everything Shastri said. Ayub was most relieved that Shastri agreed to return to India's prewar borders without insisting on any humiliating concessions from Pakistan. When the conference ended on 10 January, Ayub and Shastri shook hands warmly and signed their agreement with smiles on both faces. Bhutto glowered and withdrew scowling, then muttered that Ayub had "betrayed" Pakistan, "abandoning its just claims to Kashmir."

Immediately after this peace conference, Shastri's frail heart gave out in frozen Tashkent, and none of his doctors could resuscitate him. Awakened by his own aide and told, "The bastard is dead," Bhutto characteristically replied, "Which one?"[5]

Ayub helped carry Shastri's coffin to the plane that flew his body home. Bhutto continued to view Ayub, who had brought him into the government as the youngest member of his cabinet against the advice of several older colleagues, with great contempt. Soon after they returned to Pakistan, he embarked on a series of vitriolic public attacks on Ayub's "betrayal" of Pakistan at Tashkent. It was the start of Bhutto's own campaign for the presidency. The rhetorical scorn he hurled at Ayub won wild acclaim from crowds of Punjabis and Sindis in Lahore and Karachi. The charismatic Bhutto ripped open the buttons of his silk shirts as he roused crowds of frustrated Punjabi students and unemployed Sindis to cheer him and curse Ayub, who soon fired Bhutto from the cabinet. Bhutto then started his Pakistan People's Party (PPP), whose popular mantra promised "Bread, Clothing, and Housing" ("Roti, Kapra aur Makan") to Pakistan's impoverished masses. Bhutto's passion and promises hypnotized audiences, mobilizing young women as well as men; his wife, Nusrat, and daughter, Benazir, joined him in challenging Pakistan's wealthiest "twenty-two families" and vast landowning old guard, promising peasants, workers, and women a richer, happier, brighter future.

Riots spread across East and West Pakistan, leading Ayub to reimpose martial law early in 1969, filling Dhaka's jails and Punjab's fortress prisons with lawyers and other political prisoners. Students kept shouting, "Ayub must go!" but the field marshal seemed deaf to such protests. Then, in February, Bhutto announced his intention "to fast until death," the only time he ever followed in Mahatma Gandhi's footsteps, and three days later Ayub lifted his draconian martial law, losing heart as he faced growing calls from old friends to step down. All of Sind seemed to celebrate with songs and street dancing, shouts of "*Jiye* Bhutto!" ("Long live Bhutto!") echoing from Karachi to the North-West Frontier. Bhutto was hailed as the *Quaid-i-Azam* (leader of the people), a title he retained for the rest of his life, till that of Shaheed (martyr) was added to it when he was hanged.

On Pakistan Day, 25 March 1969, Ayub surrendered his marshal's baton, handing it down to General Aga Mohammad Yahya Khan, a much smaller Pathan, and a heavier drinker. Yahya was a boon companion of Bhutto's, often visiting the latter's huge ancestral estate in Sind's Larkana, where they hunted wild boar together and drank all night. Pressure from Washington to hold a general election mounted as the cost of America's military aid to Pakistan grew much higher than anticipated. General strikes in East Pakistan and social disorder in West Pakistan spread with such alarming speed that the country seemed ready to collapse rather than growing stronger. Yahya, therefore, agreed to preside over the transfer of power to elected representatives of the people as swiftly as possible. He insisted that he had no ambition to retain power, but in addition to his new title of chief martial law administrator, he took Ayub's title of president and remained Pakistan's top general.

Pakistan's first national elections were held on 7 December 1970, in the wake of a hurricane tidal wave that drowned a quarter of a million of East Pakistan's poorest people in the low-lying Delta of Bengal and left millions without food or shelter. This disaster was compounded by Yahya's failure to send immediate aid to the region, leaving Bengali peasants to die without food or medical supplies, which could have been flown in from West Pakistan and air-dropped to them. West Pakistan's indifference to the tragic plight of the country's eastern majority served only to further alienate Bengalis from Islamabad's ruling Punjabi and Pathan generals. When Yahya finally decided to view Bengal's devastation from his helicopter, he flew far too high to hear any of the screams or shouts of the hungry people, by then totally enraged at their West Pakistani masters, none of whom seemed to care about them, or understood their language, or tried to solve any of their problems.

FOUR

The Third Indo-Pakistani War and the Birth of Bangladesh

From its birth, Pakistan was plagued by the insoluble division of its territory into two wings, with a thousand miles of northern India between them. The Pakistan Resolution unanimously adopted by Jinnah's Muslim League in Lahore in 1940 had been drafted by a committee chaired by the League's most popular Bengali leader, A. K. Fazlul Haq. The most important section of that resolution, which never mentioned Pakistan by name, stated that

> no constitutional plan would be workable in this country [British India] or acceptable to the Muslims unless it is designed on the following basic principles, viz., that geographically contiguous units are demarcated into regions which should be so constituted, with such territorial adjustments as may be necessary, that the areas in which the Muslims are numerically in a majority, as in the North-Western and Eastern zones of India, should be *grouped to constitute Independent States* in which the constituent units shall be autonomous and sovereign.[1]

When Jinnah was asked by the press if this resolution meant one or more than one Pakistan, he immediately answered, "One!" and thus it was reported next day, in England as well as in India. There is good reason to believe, however, that Sher-i-Bengal (Lion of Bengal) Fazlul Haq had meant *two* independent states, rather than one, and that the easternmost of those "autonomous and sovereign" constituent units of British India in which Muslims were a majority was Bangladesh (the Land of Bengal). The Bangladesh that Fazlul Haq had in mind would, moreover, have included all of India's West Bengal and Calcutta, as well as what was to become East Pakistan.

Jinnah was brilliantly realistic, however, and he knew that asking for *two* independent Muslim nation-states might make the creation of Pakistan impossible. He himself was then sixty-four and physically frail, and it was no easy matter to convince not only the British, but the Indian National Congress, of the seriousness of the Muslim League's Lahore Resolution, dismissed by Congress leaders—and some British officials—as "a bargaining point," if not "the product of a diseased mentality." Though partition stripped Pakistan of the eastern half of Punjab and the western half of Bengal, including Calcutta, he therefore accepted the "moth-eaten" pieces that Mountbatten offered him.

The fragmented nation-state, split into two mutually remote wings, never really worked, however, and when Jinnah paid his first, brief, and only visit to Dhaka as Pakistan's Great Leader, he announced that West Pakistan's Urdu, rather than East Pakistan's Bengali, was to be Pakistan's sole national language. The millions of Bengalis who heard this speech needed no further evidence of their intolerably subordinate status to West Pakistan. Though they were all, indeed, Muslims, the primary bond that united them was their mother-tongue, not their religious faith. The richness and poetry of Bengali, the language of Rabindranath Tagore, was the cultural glue that made their "Golden Bengal" a nation. So in December 1970, in the wake of that year's devastating cyclone, every Bengali who voted cast his vote for Sheikh Mujibur Rahman's Awami (People's) League, whose Six Points called for the virtual independence of East Pakistan's Bangladesh from West Pakistan's military junta.

Most West Pakistanis voted for Zulfi Bhutto's Pakistan People's Party, but there were ten million fewer voters in the West than in the East, so the Awami League won 160 seats, all but two of the contests in the East, while the PPP could claim only 81 seats in the West. Mujibur Rahman should, therefore, have become Pakistan's newly elected prime minister the very day all those votes were finally counted early in 1971. Neither Zulfi Bhutto nor Yahya Khan could accept the idea of turning their entire country over to Bengalis, however, whose language neither of them spoke, and whose small, dark-skinned physiques neither of them believed worthy specimens of Pakistani stature. In many ways, West Pakistanis treated their eastern "colony" as arrogantly as British sahibs had ruled all of India. So though Pakistan's new National Assembly should have been convened in Dhaka that March, Bhutto wouldn't allow a wavering Yahya to do it, offering instead to fly east himself to cut a deal with Mujib.

In some respects, Bhutto and Mujib, both born to relish political power, were alike: passionate orators, charismatic leaders, inspiring millions to cheer for them and, if need be, to die for them. Bhutto was much richer, however, having inherited vast feudal estates in Sind, whereas Mujib had earned his first rupees in Calcutta selling insurance. Bhutto's hero was Napoleon, whose sword hung facing the gold-topped Louis XIV desk in his Karachi library. Mujib, however, looked no further for his role model than to Bengal's one and only prime minister of Pakistan, H. S. Suhrawardy. It was intolerable for Bhutto to allow such a lowborn person to became Pakistan's premier, especially now that he himself was ready to take on that job.

He first persuaded Yahya to put off convening a new National Assembly, though popular and international pressure was building daily, Delhi and Washington wondering why Yahya hadn't done so immediately. But Yahya did whatever Bhutto told him, since Zulfi was, after all, so much more sophisticated, a graduate of several colleges in California, a student of Christ Church, Oxford, a Lincoln's Inn barrister, and a wealthy Sindhi landlord. Moreover, Bhutto had a brilliant idea of how best to resolve this problem.

He flew to Dhaka in late March and offered Mujib what he considered a very generous deal: "You will be prime minister here, and I will be prime minister there!" *Two Pakistans!* Not for nothing had Bhutto mastered the works of Machiavelli at Berkeley. Only Mujib wasn't buying it. He had won the whole loaf in a free and fair election, after all; why now take only half? To every reporter in Dhaka he protested: "First they want credit for holding free elections, but now that they've lost, they want to change the rules, so they fly this Sindhi here to beg me to play their dirty game!" Bhutto was not amused. Nor was Yahya, who had flown out himself in the last week of March to close the deal, believing that the clever, suave Bhutto would surely sway this Bengali rustic to accept his offer.

On 25 March 1971, however, Yahya Khan flew home in frustration, even as the sun started to set over Bangladesh. The next morning, Bhutto followed him. Pakistan's toughest general,

Tikka Khan, ordered his West Pakistani troops to open fire that night, pointing the long guns of their American-built M24 tanks at Dhaka's crowded Hindu bazaar, opening fire on sleeping students in Dhaka University's dormitories. As Zulfi Bhutto stepped out of his plane in Karachi the next morning, he was asked by airport reporters welcoming him home what the results of his talks with Mujib had been. "By the grace of God, Pakistan has been saved," Bhutto replied.

But back in Dhaka, West Pakistani troops kept firing, and then surrounded Mujib's house, arresting him. That Dhaka massacre triggered an exodus of ten million Hindus, fleeing by every river and mud road to India's border, to refugee camps set up all around Calcutta, soon threatening to choke the very air out of that great city. The events of late March 1971 augured the birth of independent Bangladesh as a nation, reincarnated from the corpse of East Pakistan.[2]

"Dear Sisters and Brothers," began the message Mujib left his people, which was read aloud in every mango grove and village throughout Bangladesh. "You are citizens of a free country. . . . West Pakistan's military force is engaged in a genocide in Bangla Desh. . . . Allah is with us. The world public opinion is with us. *Jai Bangla!* [Victory to Bengal!]"

Shastri's death in Tashkent in 1966 had brought Nehru's daughter, Indira Gandhi, to the helm in New Delhi. Nehru had long groomed her to be prime minister, appointing her India's official national hostess and taking her with him whenever he traveled abroad to foreign capitals. Though her Parsi husband, Firoze Gandhi, was unrelated to Mahatma Gandhi, millions of Indian peasants believed that Indira Gandhi was the Mahatma's daughter, not Nehru's, adding to her uniquely popular voter appeal. Like her father, she was a socialist and a born politician, and she took a keen interest in Sheikh Mujibur Rahman, more aware of his Awami League's appeal throughout East Pakistan than most West Pakistani political leaders ever were. She also understood how easy it was for President Nixon and his alter ego, Henry Kissinger, to manipulate men like Yahya Khan and Zulfi Bhutto. How oddly fortuitous it now seemed to her that Bangladesh should suddenly become so ripe for plucking away from the clasp of the military tyrants of West Pakistan, who had tried to steal Kashmir from India little more than half a decade earlier.

Indira understood Bengali, having studied music and other arts at Rabindranath Tagore's rural Shantiniketan College, north of Calcutta. She could speak with Mujib in his own language, which brought them closer together, both before and after the birth of Bangladesh. The only Pakistani leader who understood just how close Indira Gandhi was to Mujib was Zulfi Bhutto, who told Yahya that Mujib was "Indira's puppet" before he flew to Dhaka to try to persuade Mujib to accept his plan.

Nixon's White House had ample telegraphic warnings of the Pakistani army's Dhaka massacre from the State Department's consular officer in East Pakistan, Archer Blood, who witnessed its entire horrible onset. Nixon ignored all of Blood's pleas for humanitarian aid, however, as well as his urging that there be an immediate end to U.S. arms shipments to Pakistan. "Tricky Dick" was preoccupied with his top-secret plans at this time to send Kissinger to China to meet with Chou and Mao as the prelude to his own flight to Beijing to announce U.S. recognition of the People's Republic. While Bangladesh burned and its refugees fled in terror, Kissinger flew first to Islamabad to meet with Yahya, who had set the stage for the Sino-U.S. Friendship Treaty.

Zulfi Bhutto's Sino-Pakistani Treaty of Friendship was viewed by Indira Gandhi as a highly ominous potential pincer strategy, aimed at both India's northern tier and the west of the country.

Fearing how dangerous this new U.S.-Pakistan-China alliance could be for India, Mrs. Gandhi launched her own search for international support, flying to Moscow that summer to appeal for help from the Kremlin. On 9 August 1971, Indira signed the twenty-year Treaty of Peace, Friendship, and Cooperation with the Soviet Union, giving her the superpower nuclear cover she required and the heavy military support India needed before moving its army into Bangladesh. Then, that November, she flew to Washington, appealing to Nixon and Kissinger for help to feed and clothe the ten million Bangladeshi refugees who by then ringed Calcutta. Nixon told her only to give Yahya more time to draft a new constitution for Pakistan. So she flew home and gave India's Parsi Field Marshal Sam Manekshaw and his Sikh second-in-command, Lieutenant General Jagjit Singh Aurora, the green light to move east over Bengal's border.

Heavy Soviet artillery and tanks supported India's army as it pushed into Bangladesh, shattering Pakistani resistance completely within a month. Yahya flew Bhutto to Mao and Chou to beg them for support, but they offered him nothing. Nixon sent the nuclear-armed U.S. aircraft carrier *Enterprise* from the Seventh Fleet into the Bay of Bengal, supposedly to "evacuate refugees." All he achieved by that bullying gesture was to prod Indira Gandhi into urging India's nuclear scientists to work harder to build their own atomic bombs, the first of which would be exploded three years later under Rajasthan's desert.

From China, Bhutto flew to New York, where he talked tough to the UN Security Council in mid-December, vowing that

Pakistan would "fight for a thousand years . . . to the last man!"
The next morning, the Pakistan army in Dhaka surrendered. "I
am not a rat," Bhutto told the council, tearing up the rest of his
prepared speech. "Today I am not ratting, but I am leaving your
Security Council. I find it disgraceful to my person and my country to remain here a moment longer." Then he and his daughter
Benazir rushed out of the council chamber together.

Nixon invited Bhutto to meet with him on Bebe Rebozo's
yacht in Key Biscayne the next day. Bhutto was promised full
support to save what was left of Pakistan, now that India's
treacherous "cow-bitch," as Nixon called Indira Gandhi, and her
"puppet Mujib" had "conspired" to steal most of Pakistan's population from Islamabad. Bhutto caught the next Pan Am flight
from New York to Rome, where a Pakistan International Airlines
plane was waiting to fly him home.

"My dear countrymen," President Bhutto told his defeated
people. "We have to pick up the pieces, very small pieces, but we
will make a new Pakistan, a prosperous and progressive Pakistan,
a Pakistan free of exploitation." He spoke nationwide over Pakistan's radio, in English, saying "the world is listening," knowing
that Nixon taped his every word. It was an inspirational speech,
much of it suggested to him by Kissinger. Next on his agenda was
to meet with Mujib in the West Pakistani prison to which they
had taken him from Dhaka on April Fool's Day. Bhutto tried
his best to convince Mujib that he was his friend, and that they
should now be allies, but Mujib wasn't quite ready for that as yet.
He accepted Bhutto's offer to put him on a plane to London,
from where he was flown to Delhi by the RAF. In Delhi, Mujib
met with Indira Gandhi, and then took an Indian plane home to
Dhaka, where he was hailed by millions of jubilant Bengalis as

their first prime minister and "father-friend" *(bangobandha)* of the new nation, Bangladesh.

India's victory over Pakistan in 1971 exalted the status of Indira Gandhi to heights of popularity and power never attained even by her father. Millions of Indians believed her to be nothing less than the mother goddess Durga. Throughout Europe she was admired as a great strategist and brilliant diplomat who had defeated both Pakistan and the United States at a single blow. Mujib was sworn in as prime minister in Dhaka on 10 January 1972, and by March the ten million Bangladeshis who had fled to Calcutta all returned home. Yayha was cursed by his own army for their humiliating defeat, and denounced by Bhutto as "a liar, a drunkard, and a fraud." Thus, a quarter century after it was born, Pakistan had lost more than half its original population and the respect of most of the world.

FIVE

From the Simla Summit to Zia's Coup

Bhutto was clever enough to know just how badly Pakistan had been beaten and how weak it really was, despite the brave words he used in trying to lift the spirits of his defeated countrymen. But he also knew that the fortunes and destinies of nations often change quickly, and that in some respects losing Bangladesh was a great advantage for Pakistan. Though the country's eastern wing's exports of jute had earned most of Pakistan's hard currency during their decades linked together, its ten million Hindus had always seemed to Bhutto a potential fifth column, and, indeed, all Bengalis seemed less than trustworthy to him, more like Indians than true Pakistanis, most of whom were tougher, "real" Muslims.

Bhutto decided first of all to try to convince Indira Gandhi to agree to a peace treaty to reassure his generals that India would be no further immediate problem for them, and if possible to remove the continuing conflict over Kashmir from their troubled minds. He also resolved now to work on building atomic bombs and trying to acquire the technology needed to deliver them with Pakistan's own missiles. That April, he ended martial law and announced his intention to "bring back the rule of law" to Pakistan, as a prelude to his courtship of Indira Gandhi at their Summit Peace Conference in Simla, scheduled for June 1972.

Bhutto brought his daughter Benazir to the summit among his entourage of ninety-two PPP followers and government officials. Indira Gandhi greeted them at Simla's eagle-perch airport as they stepped out of the Soviet helicopter that flew them up from Lahore. Their summit was held at the grand viceregal palace the British had built for their summer capital, with the silver crown of Himalayan ice-tops to its north. Bhutto's oldest Indian school chum, Piloo Mody, had flown in with the Indian delegation. "Bhutto . . . is above all a realist," Piloo wrote, "a great bluffer when he holds a poor hand, but always ready to arrive at mutually acceptable solutions if his opponent is big enough or shrewd enough not to push him into a corner."[1] Indira Gandhi was both. Precious little was agreed upon during the first three days, but on the fourth and last evening, after the presidents' dinner, they went off alone to agree upon the final details of their peace agreement, which they signed on 2 July 1972.

Bhutto and Gandhi agreed to "settle their differences by peaceful means through bilateral negotiations" in the future, and the UN cease-fire line in Kashmir was renamed the "Line of Control."[2] Indira would have accepted that Line of Control as Kashmir's international border if Pakistan had agreed. No mention was made of any future plebiscite in Kashmir, however, and Bhutto's opponents in Lahore denounced him for having sold out Pakistan's future claims to all of the Vale. Bhutto solemnly swore that he had promised Indira "nothing" as to the future of Kashmir, but, as Piloo noted, Bhutto was both a realist and a great bluffer. After the Simla meeting, India returned more than 5,000 square miles of Pakistani desert captured during the 1971 war, and soon agreed to allow Pakistan to have its 93,000 Bihari prisoners back, though no government in Islamabad has ever been eager to make room for so many Biharis, still unwanted by both countries.

Pakistan remained much diminished and poorer, but Bhutto now had the time he needed to forge ahead in rebuilding its power, diplomatically as well as technologically. The Simla summit restored his self-confidence and enhanced Pakistan's international stature. So Bhutto focused on what he called his nation's need to "unleash a great force," encouraging Pakistan's physicists and engineers to learn as much as possible about nuclear weapons and to buy, or steal whatever they could not purchase, from the West. Dr. A. Q. Khan was the most notorious of those Pakistani nuclear procurers, stealing plans of "the secret uranium enrichment process" by "ultracentrifugation," developed in Amsterdam's Physical Dynamics Research Laboratory, where he was employed in 1973.[3] Dr. Khan flew home with his stolen keys to the swift enrichment of uranium in December 1974, taking charge of Pakistan's Kahuta Atomic Energy Laboratory. Bhutto himself arranged to import uranium fuel from Libya, and missile technology for the delivery of nuclear-armed missiles from North Korea and China. Zulfi vowed "to eat grass" rather than to reduce the funding required by Pakistan's Atomic Energy Agency to carry out his highest new priority mission. He hoped to beat India at acquiring enough plutonium to test an atomic bomb, but India crossed that finish line much earlier than Pakistan, announcing its first underground nuclear explosion on 18 May 1974, ironically, the "birthday" of the Buddha.[4]

In 1974, Zulfi Bhutto was at the peak of his power. That year, he hosted thirty-eight heads of Islamic states in Lahore at a lavish conference whose most honored guests included King Faisal of Saudi Arabia, Presidents Hafiz al-Assad of Syria and Anwar Sadat of Egypt, Colonel Qaddafi of Libya, and Prime Minister Mujibur Rahman of Bangladesh. Bhutto's Pakistan had become the unifier of the Islamic world. China and North Korea were Pakistan's closest East Asian allies, and Bhutto proudly spoke of it as Asia's "midmost nation," with the mission of "mediating conflicts." The atomic bomb he sponsored would be an Islamic bomb, he assured both Qaddafi and Assad.

Zulfi thought of himself as a combination of Napoleon and Mao. His appetite for wine and women was as insatiable as his lust for power. Wiser compatriots cautioned him against his intoxicated outbursts of violence and threats to leave political enemies with "no legs" to stand on. Bhutto believed himself impervious to arrest, however, no matter what crimes he committed. His fatal mistake was his promotion of a seemingly unambitious junior lieutenant general to serve as Pakistan's chief of army staff (COAS).

General Zia ul-Haq was a devout and austere Muslim, a modest soldier, who had just been promoted to lieutenant general when Bhutto reached below five senior officers to elevate Zia to the post of COAS. All those senior generals were then forced to retire, shocked at Bhutto's wild choice. One of them considered Zia the army's "best sycophant"; another called him "a dark horse." Benazir called him "the devil," but that was after he had arrested and later hanged her father. Blinded by his own hubris, Bhutto never imagined that Zia, who always smiled at and bowed to him, would dare bite off the head of the leader who had so generously promoted him.

Zia waited patiently before arresting Bhutto, never contra-
dicting or refusing to obey his prime minister until 1977, when
Bhutto decided to renew his popular mandate, ordering nationwide elections. Like Nixon, Bhutto was obsessed by an irrational
need to win every election he contested by an absurd majority.
He liked to think that everyone loved him, though he knew how
many mullahs spoke out against his drinking and womanizing,
so on the eve of elections he prohibited the sale of all alcoholic
beverages and shut down every nightclub and bar in Karachi.
He even stopped the construction of a huge new casino on
Karachi's best beach, leaving its ugly gray shell of concrete to
remind everyone of how austere and faithful a Muslim he had
suddenly become. Fundamentalist Muslims of Maulana Mau-
doodi's Jamaat-i-Islami Party posed the greatest challenge to
Bhutto's PPP. He faced many weaker secular opponents as well,
but Bhutto dismissed those as "gnats."

After Bhutto's obviously dishonest victory by over 90 percent in every district of Punjab was announced, angry crowds
filled the streets of Lahore in protest, demanding that Bhutto
resign for rigging the contests and burning every ballot cast
for his opponents. Police were forced to open fire on Punjabi
crowds, killing several people and wounding many more, yet
the protests only grew louder and harsher. Several of Bhutto's
most respected generals-turned-ambassadors resigned at the
"disgrace" of his rigged reelection. Then Pakistan International
Airlines went on strike and all its flights were canceled. Railway union workers joined in growing calls for a general strike,
and the country soon came to a grinding halt. Bhutto appealed
to the Saudi ambassador to ask his "friend" the king of Saudi

Arabia for help, but no foreign power was willing to interfere on his behalf. So he turned to Zia, telling him to "restore order." Zia understood then that his once most popular political leader was finished. The irony of Bhutto's fall was that he could easily have won reelection and remained in power had he only allowed the electoral process to run its free course without the ridiculous rigging he demanded of his stooges. He was Pakistan's best-educated popular leader, yet he profligately squandered all his advantages and remarkable education.

After seizing power and arresting Bhutto, Zia promised to return to soldiering "soon," insisting that he was no politician, only a good soldier trying his best to save his country. Ayub Khan had said much the same thing at the start of his decade-long dictatorship, but unlike the secular Ayub, Zia planned to lead his nation with "guidance from God Almighty." He never forgot his daily prayers, and was eager to "restore order" and stop corrupt politicians from "looting" and wasting public property. He promised to be chief martial law administrator of Pakistan for no longer than ninety days, saying, "I am a very humble man." Bhutto naïvely believed that he could intimidate Zia into releasing him from his hill station "guest house" prison in Murree, and he threatened to "hang Zia" for having dared to arrest him, bragging about it to old party friends who were detained with him in the same bugged house. But Zia had known from the day he arrested his prime minister that either Bhutto must hang or he would. So he very carefully prepared murder charges against Bhutto, using Zulfi's own chief of security, Masood Mahmood, who gave the crucial testimony that he had personally been ordered by Bhutto to "eliminate" his most vocal political opponent. The man gunned down by Masood's killers, however, was the innocent old father of Bhutto's political opponent Ahmad Raza Kasuri. In March 1978, Bhutto was judged guilty of murder by the Punjabi majority of Zia's high court.

"Martial law is darkness at high noon," Bhutto rightly argued at his trial. "It is neither an order nor a system. . . . This form of lawlessness takes us back to the law of the jungle. . . . Force, naked and brute, moody and mad, cannot be made the sole criterion of our honour." Zia was unmoved by Bhutto's eloquence. The devout general considered all Western culture and philosophy sinful and the primary cause of Pakistan's weakness. Purity of Islamic prayers and practice alone, he believed, could save Pakistan from Shaytan's temptations—imbibing alcohol and pork, having sex with loose women, watching films and naked dancing girls, all things Zulfi Bhutto enjoyed. Zia closed his eyes and ears to every appeal for clemency from President Jimmy Carter and other humane heads of state. On 4 April 1979, Zulfikar Ali Bhutto was hanged before dawn from gallows in Rawalpindi's dark prison fortress that would be torn down by his daughter soon after she became prime minister following Zia's death.

"The longer martial law remains the shorter will be the remaining life of Pakistan," Bhutto had prophesied from his death cell.

> Pakistan is decomposing very fast. In Europe there was *Balkanization*. Here, there will be *Bangladeshization*. The process is in motion. Thanks to Zia's follies it has been accelerated. . . . If I am not a part of Pakistan, in that case Sind is not a part of Pakistan. . . . There are no nightmares more dreadful than the last days of a usurper, of a man who stabs his own benefactor. Brutus did it to Caesar. . . . For over a year and a

half I have been in solitary confinement. . . . I am the Rana
[Lord] of not only Larkana but of the whole of Pakistan, and
. . . certainly of Sind. . . . We are on a razor's edge.[5]

Had it not been for the Soviet invasion of Afghanistan in
December 1979, Zia might well have been forced to surrender
the powers he had illegally grabbed from Bhutto. Most of Pakistan's moderate leaders, many of whom had despised Bhutto long
before he was hanged, now feared and hated Zia's austere fanati-
cism much more than Bhutto's vulgarity or drunken orgies. But
the swift conquest of Kabul by heavy Soviet tanks and helicopter
gunships proved to be Zia's salvation. President Carter's offer of
$400 million in military aid was so contemptuously dismissed
by the general as "peanuts" that he suddenly became a hero to
Pakistan's army and mullahs. Then President Reagan, who had
defeated Carter in the 1980 presidential election, quickly raised
the promised U.S. aid to our new "front line ally" in the Cold
War to $10 billion, not only in tanks and planes, but also in new
Stinger missiles capable of seeking out and destroying Soviet
helicopters and tanks.

SIX

Afghanistan's Impact
on Indo-Pakistani Relations

From the dawn of Indian history, the Afghan Plateau has been a springboard to the conquest of India by martial raiders from the West. Indo-Aryan tribes first came down the Khyber and Bolan Passes over the Hindu Kush as early as 1500 B.C.E. Alexander the Great led his Macedonian army over the Khyber, crossing the Indus in 326 B.C.E., followed by Perso-Afghans, Central Asian Scythians, and Kushanas, Turks, and Mughals. The Muslim conquerors of Punjab, Kashmir, Sind, and the North-West Frontier converted Hindus of that region to Islam, or forced them to flee south. Though the British ultimately won control over the entire region, virtually all of the people in what is now called Pakistan remained Muslims. The dominant Pathan tribes of Pakistan's North-West Frontier Province speak the same Pashtun language as their Afghan neighbors and use the same frontier plateau land to graze their goats and sheep as do the Baloch tribes to their south.

Nor were the British ever able to march west over those high passes or long retain control over Afghanistan's capital, Kabul, or its second-largest city, Kandahar. Several arrogant British viceroys and generals thought they had beaten those "wily Pathans," but most never lived to return home.[1] Then, before the end of the nineteenth century, as Russia's empire moved south, the "Great Game" began between tsarist Russia and British India for control of Afghanistan's Hermit Kingdom. Tsar Peter the Great viewed Russia's expansion into Central Asia in 1710 as his "destiny" and "civilizing mission." Subsequent tsars absorbed the Muslim sultanates of Bokhara, Khiva, and Khokand into Russia's empire, lowering Russia's mid-nineteenth-century border at Tashkent and Samarkand to within a few hundred miles of British India. In 1828, when Persia opened Tehran to a Russian deputation, British strategists feared the frost of Russia's glacier advancing toward Kabul. "We have long declined to meddle with the Afghans," Britain's Lord Palmerston warned, "but if the Russians try to make them Russian, we must take care they become British."[2] A decade later British India launched its "glorious" Army of the Indus over the Khyber to take Kabul, the first of their several futile attempts to conquer Afghanistan, from which they were forced to flee in desperation three years later, all shot dead before any Anglo-Indian soldiers reached home.

So when Soviet tanks and troops moved into Kabul at the end of 1979, installing their puppet Amir Babrak Karmal as the country's nominal ruler, Washington was as alarmed as was Islamabad. Pakistan's intense anxiety was easy enough for the United States to understand, it having been engaged since the end of World War II in the Cold War with Moscow. But India's reaction to the Soviet advance was ambivalent, not only because Indira Gandhi had just recently signed her treaty of friendship with Moscow, but also since Pakistan's Zia was so aggressively a fundamentalist Muslim, eager to arm and support thousands of Pathan mujahideen (jihadist) guerrillas, backed by the CIA, the Pentagon, and the White House. Indira was reluctant, therefore, to condemn the Soviet invasion as most of the world denounced it at the United Nations, voting instead to abstain rather than to support so clear an act of international bullying. New Delhi's military leaders, however, warned Gandhi of the obvious dangers of a powerful Soviet force sitting on South Asia's vulnerable frontier, for if ever they did come rumbling down the Khyber, there was precious little to stop Soviet tanks from rolling on toward New Delhi itself, before which they might even be joined by Pakistan's army.

India's oldest text on realpolitik, the *Arthaśāstra*, early taught Delhi's monarchs that one's neighbor was always "the enemy," while one's "neighbor's neighbor" was always "the friend"—or at least should be. India and Pakistan have, therefore, long had classical adversarial roles toward Afghanistan. In the era of General Zia's rule, that conflict intensified as four million Afghan refugees poured into Pakistan, where they received not only food and shelter, but also arms from Islamabad's leaders, who viewed Indira Gandhi as the USSR's best friend in Kabul and Kandahar. Throughout the decade of Soviet dominance in Afghanistan, Pakistan, with massive U.S. military aid and money, trained tens of thousands of Islam's fiercest fighters. Initially, they were Afghan Pathans, but later many came from every Arab country, including the most infamous leaders of Al-Qaeda, Saudi Arabia's Osama bin Laden and his lieutenants. The latter were supported by the CIA as well as Pakistan's Inter-Services Intelligence (ISI) agency, through which Pakistan's army channeled billions of

Map 3.   Pakistan and Afghanistan.

dollars in money and matériel received from Washington. India soon learned that many of Afghanistan's fiercest mujahideen were Muslim terrorists who aimed to do as much damage as they possibly could to Indian Kashmir.

Zia's fundamentalist passions drove him to plan to turn Pakistan into a mullah-run society with Islam's medieval primary system of education, taught in thousands of madrassas, supported by Saudi Arabian money, to house Pakistani boys and young men, who memorized only the Qur'an and learned to use weapons for jihad against Indian and Western infidels. During his eleven years in power, Zia armed and funded those four million Afghan refugees, who lived under tents in Pakistan's North-West Frontier Province and were regularly sent back to Afghanistan to shoot down Soviet helicopters and blow up tanks and trucks. The impact of its defeat in Afghanistan on Moscow's "Evil Empire," as Reagan called the Soviet Union, helped to accelerate its collapse by the end of 1989. As long as Zia armed enough mujahideen to succeed in carrying out that highest Cold War priority for the White House, nothing dreadful he did, or failed to do, at home evoked negative reactions from Washington. He was thus left to sow seeds of global terror that would threaten the entire world little more than a decade after his own C-130 presidential plane went down in flames near Bahawalpur in Punjab on 17 August 1988.

No one ever claimed responsibility for the death of Zia's planeful of generals as well as the U.S. ambassador to Pakistan, Arnold Raphel, and one American general, both of whom had joined the flight at Zia's urgent insistence. No FBI investigation of the crash was ever made public. Most Pakistanis believe that a gift box of mangoes loaded onto the plane minutes before takeoff contained deadly poison nerve gas that killed both pilots, and that the CIA was responsible. Some believe that either the Soviet KGB or Afghan Intelligence (KAKH) had strong enough motives and capability to do the job. Still others think it was the Indian cabinet's intelligence bureau, the Research and Analysis Wing (RAW), that assassinated Zia to expedite the regime change in Islamabad that swiftly followed. On 2 December 1988, elections held throughout Pakistan by its new president, Ghulam Ishaq Khan, brought Benazir Bhutto's PPP to power. She was sworn in as Pakistan's first female prime minister.

Four years before Benazir's rise to premier power, Indira Gandhi had been gunned down in her own garden by two of her trusted Sikh bodyguards. The tragic assassination of Nehru's daughter on 31 October 1984 was triggered by the Indian army's "Operation Bluestar," a tank attack launched against Amritsar's Golden Temple that Gandhi had authorized early that June. Armed Sikh extremists had taken control of the temple and its sacred tower repository of Sikh scripture, demanding a separate Sikh state of Khalistan (Land of the Pure), humiliating Indira Gandhi and her administration with their taunts and treacherous challenges. She should have known better than to send tanks into that most sacred temple compound, but it was an election year, and her Congress Party MPs feared that if she continued to look too weak to crush the Khalistan extremists occupying the temple, they would all surely be defeated.

The outpouring of nationwide sympathy following Indira's death assured the Congress Party, led by Indira's son Rajiv, its strongest historic victory. Zia had flown to Delhi to meet with Rajiv at Indira Gandhi's funeral, and saw him there again in December 1985, after the first meeting of the South Asian Association for Regional Cooperation (SAARC) in Dhaka in Bangladesh, when they agreed not to attack each other's nuclear installations. That promising start to a hopeful process of South Asian reconciliation was followed, however, by a futile series of five rounds of talks on the deadly conflict over the Siachen Glacier, Kashmir's highest frozen peak, just east of the Line of Control.[3] Since 1984, when the Indian army first occupied these heights, thousands of Indian and Pakistani soldiers have died fighting over the glacier. Uncounted amounts of money have been wasted by both sides in exchanging heavy artillery fire over it.

Soon after Benazir was elected, she met with Rajiv for a two-day summit in Islamabad in June 1989. These youthful heirs to dynastic power, both of the same generation, appeared to like each other. Had they remained in high office longer, and lived long enough, they might well have reached diplomatic agreements on how best to stop fighting over frozen wastelands like Siachen, squandering their nations' most preciously valuable resources in Kashmir, and built instead "on the progress in Pakistan-Indian relations our parents had established in the Simla Accord," as Benazir Bhutto much later wisely noted.[4]

But Rajiv Gandhi failed to take swift advantage of the wave of popularity and sympathy that had lifted him to the peak of Indian power, and he soon lost his reputation as "Mr. Clean," allowing two very promising accords he had reached with popular leaders of Punjab and Assam to lapse for lack of initiative as well as energy. He tried to end the Sri Lankan civil war by sending an Indian peacekeeping force to Jaffna, but that mission also failed. Then, on the eve of what might well have been his Congress Party's reelection to power in 1991, Rajiv Gandhi was assassinated by a Tamil Tiger terrorist woman while campaigning near Madras.

Benazir lost the confidence of Pakistan's leaders of the all-powerful ISI, Generals Hamid Gul and Durrani, who viewed her as "too soft" toward India, realizing that like her father she was ready to accept the Line of Control as the international border. The ISI invested heavily in undermining her PPP's majority, until new elections were called less than two years after Benazir had taken power, and in October 1990 her party lost to a more militant Islamic coalition led by Kashmir-born Nawaz Sharif of Punjab, who replaced her as prime minister. The base of Bhutto's political power was Sind, but until her cordial meeting with

Rajiv, many Punjabis of Lahore had also strongly supported Benazir. After a concerted negative campaign against her and her "Mr. 10 Percent" husband, Asif Ali Zardari, who was arrested on charges of corruption, most Pakistanis lost faith in "that Woman." Nawaz, however, proved less capable than Benazir of winning vital international support for Pakistan's deteriorating economy, retaining his power for only a few years before he was removed by Pakistan's president, who brought Benazir back for a second term in 1993.

With the Soviet forces driven out of Afghanistan by then, and no further U.S. funding in the pipeline for Pakistan, Afghanistan reverted to its traditional tribally fragmented feudal state. A new militant force of extremist Muslim "students"—Pashto *ṭālibān*— emerged to take control of Kandahar by the end of 1994, most of them Pathans of former jihadist groups who had lost their financial support.[5] Taliban terrorists with Kalashnikov rifles violently imposed their fundamentalist views of Islamic Sharia law on Afghan women and men, never hesitating to kill those who dared to dispute their authority. Their one-eyed leader, Mullah Omar, ordered the destruction of magnificent gigantic ancient stone Buddhist statues at Bamiyan, which for more than a thousand years had lured tourists from every part of the world to Afghanistan. Benazir supported popular Taliban-run madrassas in Pakistan, all of which paid their own way, mostly through funds from Saudi Arabia. She also urged President Clinton to support the Taliban, who were then competing against Iran's favorite warlords for the control of Afghanistan. Before the end of 1996, Taliban forces had captured Kabul and hanged its former Soviet puppet ruler, Amir Najibullah, while the Tajik warlord Ahmad Shah Masud fled north from that captured capital.

Taliban rule in Afghanistan enforced banning women from public work, closing down every female school and college in Kabul, imposing Islam's veiled dress code on the entire female population, cutting off the hands of thieves, and publicly stoning adulterers. Music was banned from the airwaves and men without beards were subject to arrest. Afghanistan reverted to a medieval Islamic tribal polity. The Uzbek warlord General Rashid Dostum's men joined forces with Masud's Tajiks in opposition, both strongly supported by Russia (after 1990) and India.

Benazir Bhutto's second premiership expired in November 1996, and Nawaz Sharif was returned to the top of Islamabad's slippery pole. Nawaz also strongly supported Taliban forces, Pakistan first granting its recognition to Mullah Omar's fundamentalist regime, then urging Saudi Arabia and the United Arab Emirates to do the same. Had Nawaz and Benazir only been able to work together, trying to reconcile their personal differences and deep suspicions of each other, Pakistan might have been saved its prolonged return to military rule. But neither leader trusted the other, leaving both vulnerable to easy removal by the army. Nawaz believed Benazir to be India's tool on the question of Kashmir and was more reluctant himself to consider the idea of agreeing to treat the Line of Control as the Indo-Pakistani border. Obsessed as he became with fears of how soft Benazir was toward India, Sharif failed to realize that to Pakistan's ISI and its generals, he was also viewed as too weak to govern.

After the withdrawal of Soviet forces, Afghanistan reverted to a medieval state under Taliban-led tyranny. In Kashmir, a new era of insurgency and terror began, with cries of "Azaadi!" ("Freedom!") echoing across its beautiful valley and to the frozen top of the embattled Siachen Glacier.

SEVEN

Pakistan's Proxy War
and Kashmir's *Azaadi* Revolution

With no Soviet troops left to fight in Afghanistan, Pakistan's ISI vigorously focused its attention on Kashmir, encouraging unemployed mujahideen to help them liberate it from the steel grip of India's strongly entrenched army in the Vale. Indira Gandhi's last decade in power had proved as tragic for Kashmir as it did for Punjab. Her victory over Pakistan in the Bangladesh War and the success of India's first plutonium explosion in 1974 had raised her to so powerful a position, not only in New Delhi but throughout the world, that Indira Gandhi seemed to have lost her judgment, and certainly her patience with any opposition. She behaved as though she considered herself omniscient, and listened more to the rash and foolish advice of her ambitious younger son, Sanjay, than to any of her father's old friends and wisest advisers, like Jaya Prakash Narayan and Morarji Desai. Thus, in 1975, when Allahabad's High Court found her guilty of campaign malpractice, a crime that should have barred her from elective office for six years, instead of handing over her powers to senior colleagues in her own Congress Party, at least until the Supreme Court could decide her appeal, Gandhi suspended India's Constitution, declaring a national "Emergency." All opposition parties and papers were banned, leaders were arrested, and every prison in India was filled with courageous freedom-fighters who had, like her own father, been treated much the same way by British imperial rulers.

Indira Gandhi's injudicious reaction to her conviction aroused India's best and bravest voices against her harsh dictatorship and tyranny, awakening Kashmir's young men and women, much as it did their contemporaries in every other state of India's Union. With more than half a million Indian troops and paramilitary police based in the Vale of Kashmir by 1975, that state looked more like an occupied territory than part of a free country. Every fine hotel in Srinagar was usurped by the Indian army to house and feed its officers, as were the best houseboats on Dal Lake. Most of India's troops in Kashmir were Hindus from the south or from remote regions of the land who understood neither the Kashmiri language nor the Islamic faith, and many of whom had never before met any Muslims. Major crossroads of Srinagar were blocked by sandbag towers erected in their centers with anxious soldiers inside, peering out from behind automatic weapons at even more anxious pedestrians and slow-moving traffic. Hardly a day passed without some incident that led to either the arrest or shooting deaths of young Kashmiris, who bravely shouted or innocently laughed at seeing those soldiers trembling behind their deadly weapons.

Indira Gandhi's choice for Kashmir's governor was a Hindu named Jagmohan, an autocratic sycophant who bought off enough of Dr. Farooq Abdullah's supporters in Kashmir's Assembly to undermine Farooq's elected position as chief minister of the state, triggering vocal popular opposition, which was violently repressed by Jagmohan's "black cat" Border Security guards. Lion of Kashmir Sheikh Abdullah's son Farooq was later returned to his rightful position as chief minister by Indira's son Rajiv after he inherited his mother's power in 1986. By then, however, Farooq's bravest young followers were completely alienated from him and from India, hating Jagmohan's repression and Indira Gandhi's duplicity.

The battle cry of young Kashmiris became "Azaadi!" ("Freedom!"). Had that not, after all, been the noble cry throughout India in the last decades of the British Raj? And was it not the cry that finally forced Prime Minister Gandhi herself to give up the ill-advised repression of her Emergency Raj after two years of locking up innocent opponents? Was it not the very cry suddenly sweeping the world, this cry for freedom, liberation, human rights? Why should Kashmir alone be excluded from this universal dream?

When fresh elections were held in Kashmir in 1987, a coalition of Farooq Abdullah's National Conference Party and Rajiv Gandhi's Congress Party won a clear majority in the state Assembly. "If I want to implement programmes to fight poverty, and run a government, I will have to stay on the right side of the center," the realist Farooq explained to reporters.[1] Kashmir's most ardent Muslim youth, however, viewed Farooq's realism as cowardice or capitulation to New Delhi's pressures and temptations, joining together in a Muslim United Front, including the Jamaat-i-Islami and other Islamic fundamentalist groups led by the popular Kashmiri preachers Qazi Nissar and Maulvi Abbas Ansari. The rigging of elections in 1987 proved so blatant that many of Kashmir's most popular young Muslims, like Abdul Ghani Lone, lost their bids for Assembly seats only because police arrested most of their followers at polling stations, persuading young idealists to turn to bullets after seeing the ballot fail them. Pakistan's ISI was ready to help train those young Kashmiris in any and every way possible, offering them weapons and exercises in urban insurrection, eager to undermine India's power in the Vale of Kashmir at such relatively little expense to themselves.

In December 1989, the daughter of Kashmiri Home Minister Mufti Mohammad Sayeed was kidnapped by several members of the Jammu and Kashmir Liberation Front (JKLF), who demanded the release of all their leaders from prison in return for her life. Foreign Minister Inder Kumar Gujral flew to Srinagar to arrange for Rubaiya Sayeed's release. Her safe return was warmly welcomed by most members of the government in Delhi, though some now view it as "abject surrender" to Kashmiri "militants," which only helped to make them bolder in later actions and demands.[2] In 1990, Jagmohan was flown back to Srinagar as Kashmir's governor, inducing Chief Minister Farooq to resign immediately, launching a second, harsher phase of official terror throughout the Vale. Jagmohan insisted that the bullet was the "only solution" for Kashmir's militants, ordering his troops to fire at anyone daring to break his curfew or violate his draconian orders. The former happy valley returned to its darkest night of fear and terror. Hindu pandits and moderate Muslims fled from "the Wounded Valley."[3] The Indian flag was raised over an empty central square in Srinagar, guarded by heavily armed troops on Republic Day, 26 January 1992, symbolizing the total alienation of Kashmiris from New Delhi's autocratic regime.

Four young Muslim freedom-fighters had now emerged in Srinagar as the most popular leaders of Kashmir: Hamid Sheikh, Ashfaq Wani, Javed Mir, and Yasin Malik. Ashfaq Wani, a member of the Jammu and Kashmir Liberation Front, was only twenty-three when he was gunned down by Indian soldiers in March 1990. His coffin was followed by half a million silent mourners who ignored curfew orders to remain indoors, marching defiantly behind the body to Srinagar's cemetery. Thousands of young men vowed to follow Ashfaq's example in the swelling ranks of Kashmir's Azaadi fighters. Kalashnikov rifles and military training were provided to JKLF mujahideen in Azad Kashmir, and most of these young fighters optimistically believed India would soon be forced to relax its grip in frustration at the growing signs and sounds of violent opposition that spread across the Vale. Some imagined that Pakistan would attack first to help liberate them. Neither happened. The more resisters emerged in the heyday of this revolution, the more their leaders disagreed over tactics and strategy instead of uniting behind a single respected head or council of like-minded Azaadis. Several promising attempts were made to unify the competing Azaadis, the best of which was the creation of the All-Parties Hurriyat (Liberation) Conference (APHC), which brought together over thirty leaders.

Pakistan's ISI paid and trained the most militant Islamic fundamentalists sent across the Line of Control, members of Hafiz M. Sayeed's Lashkar-e-Taiyba (LeT), who attacked as many Indians and their Kashmiri collaborators as they could in Srinagar. That swiftly changed the nature of what had begun as an Azaadi revolution into a terrorist jihadi movement. Indian police and soldiers in Kashmir retaliated in kind, armed with draconian new powers under the Special Powers and Terrorism Acts and

Disruptive Activities (Prevention) Acts to "shoot on sight" any-one suspected of "disloyal" activities. The number of Kashmiris killed in the Vale escalated rapidly, but in addition to numerous Muslim deaths, most of the politically influential Hindu pandit population of Kashmir, which in 1989 was estimated to number 130,000, were driven out of the Vale and terrorized to flee south to Jammu, where many still must live in crowded, filthy refugee camps without privacy or adequate medical care.

India launched its most intense counterinsurgency catch-and-kill strategy in Kashmir in the early 1990s. Tens of thousands of young Kashmiris "disappeared" from the Vale by 1994, many of them caught by LeT terrorists and another ISI-trained group of armed Muslims, Hizb-ul-Mujahideen (HM). As bloodshed spread through every alley and lane of Srinagar, older Kashmiris turned hostile to the revolt they had initially supported. Inno-cents were daily gunned down in the lethal cross-fire between troops and terrorists. Criminals and thugs joined the Azaadi revolt, which gave them courage and excuses to steal food and vital supplies from respectable store owners, who shook their heads in disgust at this new definition of "freedom."

Kashmir's beloved religious leader Mirwaiz Qazi Nissar was murdered in his own home in Srinagar by HM terrorists in mid-1994. His funeral was followed by a general strike throughout the Vale, tens of thousands of mourners calling upon Pakistan to stay out of Kashmir. New Delhi felt confident enough by May 1995 to plan to hold an election in Kashmir, which it said would serve as a plebiscite supporting India's continued claim to Kash-mir as an integral part of its union. Before that election could begin, however, the sacred Sufi shrine of Sheikh Nooruddin

Noorani in Charar-i-Sharief was destroyed by flames, reviving Kashmiri opposition to India's occupation army and putting New Delhi's electoral plans on hold. A few months later, five Western climbers in Kashmir were kidnapped. One, a Norwegian, was beheaded by Lashkar killers. A young American ran away fast enough to escape, but none of the others has been heard from since. Tourism and mountain climbing in Kashmir thus came to a bone-chilling end.

By mid-1995, therefore, the Azaadi revolution in the Vale had cooled down, though a thousand or so "guerrilla" terrorists continued to be listed every year by Indian officials as killed during attacks aimed at Indian soldiers. Stalls and shops in Kashmir reopened, and handicraft production slowly started to revive throughout Srinagar and other cities. In September 1996, India sponsored statewide elections, and Farooq Abdullah was returned to power as chief minister with a two-thirds majority, despite the electoral boycott against him launched by Hurriyat Conference leaders. Charges of electoral fraud were raised by some opponents, and Farooq condemned by his enemies as a motorcycle clown because he liked to drive fast around Srinagar on his own motorbike. Others denounced him as a stooge and tool of New Delhi, but none could deny he was Kashmiri, and that his state government was, in fact, the product of ballots, not bullets.

Indian official records assert that 13,000 Kashmiri "guerrillas" were killed between 1990 and 1995, but Kashmiri resistance groups themselves have claimed that no fewer than 50,000 of them died during this half decade at the height of the Azaadi revolution. The more accurate count may be somewhere between those two. The calm that followed in the Vale was as much a product of exhaustion and exasperation on the part of many Kashmiris as of their willingness to postpone the dream of Azaadi. Few Kashmiris liked having to live in an armed camp in their very own capital, yet fewer still, probably, would prefer to see all of India's troops go south if that meant opening the floodgates of terror to Pakistani-trained guerrillas, inviting them to return with automatic rifles and suicide bombers.

EIGHT

Recent Attempts to Resolve the Escalating Conflict

Prolonged secret efforts by India and Pakistan to develop nuclear weapons reached their dramatic fruition, to the anxious concern of the rest of the world, in May 1998. On 11 May, India triggered three powerful nuclear bombs under the same portion of the Rajasthan desert in which it had first exploded a single bomb twenty-four years earlier.[1] Two more bombs were exploded at the same underground station two days after the first three, sending greater shock waves rumbling through India's desert sands, rattling Pakistan's former capital of Karachi. India's Prime Minister Atul Bihari Vajpayee, whose Hindu-first Bharatiya Janata Party (BJP) had just a few months earlier come to power in New Delhi for the first time, exulted over these powerful bomb blasts. Pakistan's Prime Minister Nawaz Sharif, however, remained ominously silent.

Two weeks later, Sharif joyfully announced to the world, "We have paid them back," reporting that five Pakistani nuclear bombs had been successfully exploded under the barren hills of Baluchistan.[2] Indo-Pakistani conflicts thus suddenly escalated from the not inconsiderable dangers of conventional warfare to the terrifying new heights of potential nuclear confrontation, immediately threatening more than a billion South Asians with residual deadly clouds of nuclear pollution, ultimately capable of endangering every life on earth.

President Clinton reacted strongly, freezing all high-tech exports from the United States to both India and Pakistan, as well as any shipments of arms or military spare parts. It was, however, too late. Many of India's scientists felt confident enough to forge ahead with their nuclear and ballistic missile plans without U.S. aid, and Pakistani scientists felt almost as optimistic in pushing their Islamic bomb agenda under Dr. A. Q. Khan's direction at the Kahuta Research Laboratory. To the rest of the world, however, the prospect of any exchange of nuclear missiles between the two neighbors, whose deadliest weapons could reach each other's capitals and major cities in less than ten minutes, was too terrifying to contemplate.[3]

So most world leaders, British, Russian, and Chinese, as well as American, tried their best to persuade both Vajpayee and Sharif to reach peaceful agreements on all outstanding Indo-Pakistani conflicts as swiftly as possible. Prime Minister Vajpayee took the hopeful initiative, therefore, in February 1999 of driving across Punjab's border at Wagah to meet with Prime Minister Sharif in Lahore.

That "Spring Summit of Friendship" between Vajpayee and Sharif was greeted with black flags by thousands of angry militant Pakistanis, who cursed both leaders and did their worst to darken horizons that had briefly looked bright over Lahore's heavy old Mughal fortress. The two leaders did their best, however, to present cheerful faces to the press, agreeing to seek in a series of future meetings to resolve all outstanding disputes, including the thorniest—the conflict over Jammu and Kashmir. It almost sounded too good to be true, and soon after Vajpayee returned home to his heavily burdened desk in New Delhi, he was outraged to hear of Pakistani aggression in the northern Kashmir region of Kargil.

General Pervez Musharraf, who had been elevated to chief of army staff (COAS) by Nawaz Sharif in October 1998, prided himself on his martial daring and tactical boldness in the field. Hence, without informing his prime minister, Musharraf took it upon himself to order Pakistani troops to occupy icy Indian-built bunkers on the Line of Control in Kargil; these were occupied by Indian troops for most of the year and vacated by them only during the coldest months of each winter. As soon as Vajpayee learned of this treacherous move, he called Sharif on their hotline, angrily demanding an explanation of what had inspired such a blatant violation of the Indo-Pakistani Simla Summit Accord. Sharif protested complete ignorance of the move, however, insisting that the army had acted without his prior knowledge or authorization.

As the ice began to melt in Kargil that June, India started to attack the occupied bunkers with heavy artillery, troops, and planes, and by mid-July, Pakistan had lost more than a thousand men. Soon Vajpayee proclaimed India's victory to cheering crowds in New Delhi. President Clinton invited both prime ministers to the White House in early July, but only Sharif accepted the invitation, flying into Washington on 4 July. Clinton told him in no uncertain terms that unless Pakistan pulled all of its troops back from the Line of Control in Kargil and kept them out of the Indian bunkers, the United States would not be able to stop India from "escalating" the war. Sharif got the message and flew home to order Musharraf to keep his forces clear of the Line of Control and never to send any more soldiers up there without prior approval from his prime minister. An immediate cease-fire put an end to the Kargil war on 16 July 1999, defusing any potential nuclear escalation.

Musharraf never forgave Sharif for his "cowardice" in surrendering to U.S. pressure over Kargil, but he waited until 12 October before launching his coup to remove the prime minister from office on grounds of treason. In a memoir he published seven years later, Musharraf insisted that Sharif had launched a "coup" against *him*, referring to his own military coup as a "countercoup."[4] Musharraf charged Nawaz with attempting to murder him by denying the pilot of a plane in which he was flying home from Sri Lanka permission to land at Karachi airport. Musharraf's troops had then seized the airport, bringing their COAS home. Prime Minister Sharif was instantly arrested, tried, and found guilty by a kangaroo court, which sentenced him to death. More sensitive than Zia ul-Haq had been to international appeals for clemency, however, Musharraf permitted Sharif to fly off to Saudi Arabia with his family, after he had agreed not to run for any elective office again for at least ten years.

Musharraf first proclaimed himself chief executive of Pakistan, feeling perhaps that this was a more appealing title than chief martial law administrator. But he soon replaced it with president, while keeping his COAS rank, the true key to his power. Unlike Zia, Musharraf was neither an Islamic fundamentalist nor a religious zealot. He claimed that he was simply a good

soldier and had seized power merely to clean ɩ
"corruption" that had plunged Pakistan into
He insisted, moreover, as Ayub and Zia haḍ
was eager to return to his job of soldiering, having ...
est" in politics. Initially, most Pakistanis believed Musharraf and
admired him for trying to save their poor nation from totally
collapsing after a decade of political floundering under Benazir Bhutto and Nawaz Sharif, who kept replacing each other as
prime minister while failing to fix the economy or improve the
lot of their people.

The very week that Musharraf launched his coup, 650 million
Indians went peacefully to voting stations nationwide, reelecting
Prime Minister Vajpayee's BJP-led coalition. Never before had
the polar differences between India's robust democracy and Pakistan's inability to extricate itself from dependence on dictatorial
military dominance been so clear. Vajpayee's Foreign Minister
Jaswant Singh cautioned U.S. Deputy Secretary of State Strobe
Talbott that Islamic forces of "destabilization and disintegra-
tion" were turning Pakistan into "a failed state."[5] Talbott feared,
however, that as long as such "utter pessimism" about Pakistan
dominated thinking in New Delhi, there could be little hope of
India exercising a positive influence over Islamabad. Without
democratic India's assistance and support, Pakistan would only
slip more easily into the hands of Muslim terrorists. It had never
been more urgently important for India and Pakistan to resolve
their festering conflicts. The best estimates of global intelligence
agencies indicated that Pakistan had plutonium enough to arm
between 60 and 100 nuclear warheads. Yet no Westerners were
certain as to where those warheads were stored, or whether they
were secure from potentially falling into the hands of Al-Qaeda

or Taliban terrorists, who were active throughout most of Pakistan's volatile frontier.

Four decades of a "mutually assured destruction" (MAD) Cold War nuclear standoff between the United States and the Soviet Union had served to dispel most fears of nuclear war, which had come to be regarded as highly "unlikely." Those superpowers, however, were more remote from each other than India and Pakistan, and they had developed many more nuclear safeguards and effective early-warning systems than have as yet been introduced or mutually accepted in South Asia. Several leading Indian and Pakistani general officers, moreover, have at times argued in favor of "preventive war" against their closest neighbor, even after having crossed the nuclear threshold. In 1986, India's boldest chief of army staff, General Krishnaswamy Sundarji, launched a provocative year-long military "exercise"—"Brasstacks"—together with a land, sea, and air military "operation"—"Trident"—that engaged so many Indian forces so close to Pakistan's mid-border that the Pakistani army went on red alert.[6] Many students of Brasstacks believed Sundarji's "exercise" was actually designed to provoke a Pakistani attack, which could then be answered by a "decapitating" Indian nuclear strike against Pakistan. Sundarji revealed his frustrations in *Blind Men of Hindoostan*, his "fictionalised narrative" about an Indo-Pakistani nuclear war, by which he hoped to persuade the government of India "to institutionalise strategic policy making."[7] On Pakistan's side, Musharraf's reckless launching of the Kargil war a few years after Brasstacks might have led to nuclear war had Prime Minister Sharif been as reckless as his COAS.

Soon after the dawn of the new millennium, on 11 September 2001, New York City suffered diabolically unparalleled terrorist attacks. The minds that conceived of and coordinated those assaults on the symbols of world trade and cooperation were Al-Qaeda Saudi Muslims living in Afghanistan as the guests of Mullah Omar. The devastating damage and terror ignited on that day of darkness could have been magnified thousands of times had nuclear bombs been added to those hijacked planes.

Just as the Soviet invasion of Afghanistan little more than a decade earlier had, with massive infusions of U.S. aid, saved Zia's regime from collapsing of its own ineptitude, Pervez Musharraf's decision to join the U.S. "war" against terror, in response to Secretary of State Colin Powell's warning not to hesitate, saved his regime from bankruptcy, bringing a fresh influx of $10 billion in new weapons to America's revived front-line ally. The tragedy, however, was that the new regime in Washington, led by George W. Bush and Dick Cheney, abandoned the fight against Al-Qaeda before its leaders could be caught or killed in their Pakistani caves under the North-West Frontier, instead sending U.S. troops to fight and die in their ill-fated wasteful war in Iraq. Just when the entire world most strongly sympathized with the United States and stood ready to do everything possible to crush the threat to world peace posed by Al-Qaeda, Bush withdrew from the Afghan-Pakistani Waziristan border special U.S. forces closing in on Osama bin Laden and his followers, ordering them instead into the quagmire of Iraq. A misguided cabal of White House and Pentagon-led neoconservatives, intoxicated with oil, in this way caused much tragic damage to the world and countless deaths.

Prime Minister Vajpayee immediately offered India's support to Washington's new global struggle against terror, but since Pakistan was much closer to Afghanistan, the major support base of Osama bin Laden's followers, bolstered by Mullah Omar's Taliban, New Delhi's offer was turned down in favor of General Musharraf's. India was, therefore, obliged to watch with reawakened and growing anxiety as fresh American arms poured into the port of Karachi and were flown to every major airfield in Pakistan, reviving dreadful memories of what had happened to similar missiles and bombs left in the hands of terrorists after the Soviet army exited Afghanistan.[8] Millions of Pathans sharing wild frontier regions between Pakistan and Afghanistan once again became the recipients of guns and bombs that would soon be turned against the troops of the nations that supplied them. As Musharraf himself put it in his memoir: "I believe that our greatest oversight was to forget that when you help to organize and use people fired by extraordinary religious or ideological zeal to achieve your objectives, you must consider that they might be using you to achieve their objectives."[9] More Muslim terrorists now live in Pakistan than in any other nation, despite repeated vows to arrest or expel all of them, and in spite of several major army attacks aimed at eliminating extremist fundamentalist madrassas like the Red School in Islamabad, where thousands of young jihadis were trained.

On 13 December 2001, a car full of armed Pakistanis crashed through a gate of the Lok Sabha (House of the People) in New Delhi, where 500 of India's elected leaders, including Prime Minister Vajpayee and his entire cabinet, sat assembled. Indian police managed to kill those Pakistani terrorists before any of them could enter the heart of India's democratic parliament, though nine guards died in the exchange of fire. For the next six months, however, India's huge army, on red alert, moved closer to the Line of Control in Kashmir, as did Pakistan's smaller force. The two nuclear powers thus faced each other eyeball to eyeball till mid-June 2002, posing the greatest prolonged potential danger to South Asia as a whole, and to world peace, since the Kargil war.

General Powell immediately flew to India to appeal to Vajpayee and his cabinet to exercise greater restraint in its response, but it was only after June 2002, when the State Department pronounced India "too dangerous" for American tourists, and after General Electric and several other multinationals with heavy investments in India withdrew their office staffs and capital from New Delhi for fear of possible nuclear war, that India decided to pull back its troops. Billions of dollars in corporate investments had helped to spark India's recent economic miracle of rapid development as it vigorously embraced global enterprise, and India was sensitive to foreign fears now endangering not only its tourist industry but also future growth. Pakistan quickly followed India's pullback of forces from the Line of Control, defusing the worst crisis of the new millennium.

Yet Pakistan itself continued to fall deeper into a state of fundamentalist violence. In February 2002, Daniel Pearl, a young *Wall Street Journal* reporter who had flown to Pakistan on assignment, was kidnapped in Karachi and beheaded by terrorists with Al-Qaeda and Taliban training. General Musharraf and his army were unable to track down the killers fast enough, leaving the world aghast at how dangerous a country Pakistan had become, and how impossible it was to ensure the safety of even the most well-connected foreigners in cities as poor and crowded as Karachi. In his first address to Karachi's Legislative Assembly, Pakistan's Great Leader Jinnah had cautioned his countrymen that "the first duty of a Government is to maintain law and order,"[10] but after more than half a century, Pakistan appeared to have forgotten that wise advice.

How could so many billions in American dollars be poured into a country without requiring its recipients to invest even the smallest portion of it in measures of civil security and institution-building, sponsoring enough modern secular education to teach its police and its army at least how best to take effective action against criminals? Pearl's killers were eventually caught, several of them tried, one even sentenced to death, but that verdict remains under appeal. "How did we reach the present-day epidemic of terrorism and extremism?" Musharraf asks in his memoir, blaming the Soviet invasion of Afghanistan and its aftermath, which triggered the influx of so many Pathan refugees into Pakistan camps. Benazir Bhutto, however, blamed Musharraf himself and his military aides. Others blame Pakistan's feudal polity in Punjab and Sind, where great landowners still rule tens of thousands of serfs, who remain virtual slaves to their plows, while all along Pakistan's frontier armed Pathan and Balochi tribals remain restive, blaming their own government for failing to support them.

It is high time for Pakistan to move beyond the blame game into an era of comprehensive institutional change that starts with education and will ultimately lead to civil security and a political climate more conducive to economic development.

NINE

The Stalled Peace Process

In December 2003, Prime Minister Vajpayee met President General Musharraf on the eve of their annual session of the South Asian Association for Regional Cooperation (SAARC) in Islamabad, agreeing to a cease-fire along the Line of Control in Kashmir. This important agreement launched the composite peace process for South Asia, designed to put an end to all major conflicts between India and Pakistan. Several positive measures have since been agreed upon, the most symbolically encouraging of which is the Peace Bus that started to travel between Srinagar and Muzaffarabad in 2005, filled with happy Kashmiris, many of whom had not seen their closest relatives for half a century. Significant progress was, it seemed, also made toward agreements to pull all troops off the Siachen Glacier and out of Sir Creek in 2006, though the Indian army stubbornly blocked both of those important resolutions.

Even as this comprehensive peace process inched forward, however, suicide bombers trained by Lashkar-e-Tayiba launched a new series of attacks against India, killing 160 on Mumbai's commuter trains and blowing up buses taking Pakistanis home to Lahore and Islamabad. In Baluchistan, Pakistan's largest and still most turbulent province, eighty-year-old Nawab Akbar Bugti, the region's most popular leader, a friend of Benazir Bhutto, was shot dead inside his own home in Quetta by Pakistani troops on 26 August 2006. Some 170 Baloch "activists" have disappeared since 2000, Pakistan's Human Rights Commission reported, most of them abducted and probably killed by Pakistan's "security forces." Small wonder that Baluchistan has become the home of so many Taliban militants, including perhaps one-eyed Afghan Mullah Omar himself, as well as Balochi separatists.

General Musharraf was eager to win reelection as president in 2007, but feared that Chief Justice Iftikhar Mohammed Chaudhry might try to prevent him from doing so as long as he retained his uniform as chief of army staff. The courageous chief justice, moreover, had issued legal orders to release many innocent Pakistanis held without cause by police, so Musharraf decided to fire him in March 2007, charging Chaudhry with corruption. This autocratic act provoked immediate uproars from Pakistan's prestigious bar associations, first in Lahore, then in Karachi and Islamabad, with thousands of irate, well-attired lawyers, trained to follow in Barrister Jinnah's fearless footsteps, marching in outraged protests provoked by the general's arrogant attempt to decapitate their Supreme Court.

The increasingly popular lawyers' protest marches that followed Musharraf's reckless act proved so effective in spearheading opposition to martial rule that it soon became clear, even to Musharraf himself, that elective civil government must be restored or Pakistan would face civil war and imminent collapse.

So Musharraf met with Benazir Bhutto in Dubai, reaching a power-sharing agreement with her that would have allowed him to retain the position of president provided he surrendered his uniform. Benazir had earlier met and reached agreement with Nawaz Sharif in London, even signing a democratic elective accord with him that seemed far more promising, but, unfortunately, was then abandoned by her. Their old antipathy was never to be reconciled. Benazir distrusted Nawaz, and she thought she would have greater freedom to do as she liked working with Musharraf, but she thus left herself at the mercy of the army.

In September 2007, thousands of angry lawyers rallied to march through Islamabad, shouting, "Go, Musharraf, go!" The general still hoped, however, to hang on for another five years as Pakistan's president, and he was reelected October 6, even though he retained his uniform. Twelve days later, Benazir flew home to Karachi after eight years in exile, following Musharraf's grant of immunity to her and her husband, Asif Ali Zardari, which canceled all charges of corruption and murder previously posted against them. Millions of cheering admirers welcomed Benazir home, but the crowd was so huge, and her procession moved so slowly, that night fell before she could reach her Karachi beach house. Then the streetlights went out, and two bombs exploded directly beside her armored truck. If Benazir had not just bent down inside the steel-shelled vehicle, she would have been killed instantly, as were 179 of her supporters outside the van. She had been warned of possible assassins awaiting her return, but Zulfi Bhutto's daughter had always been fearless, fatalistically believing, "I will be safe until my time is up."

Violence spread across Pakistan in the aftermath of that first attack aimed at Benazir Bhutto, and Musharraf postponed elections scheduled in January for one month. Before year's end, political campaigns were in full swing, however, and it seemed clear from the size of the crowds that gathered to cheer Benazir that she and her father's PPP would be returned to power. After finishing a warmly received speech in Rawalpindi on 27 December 2007, Benazir stood up in her car as it drove out of the crowd and was shot dead by a young assassin, who appears to have acted on orders from Pakistan's arch-terrorist Taliban leader Baitullah Mehsud. No Pakistani could forget, of course, that in the Army Stadium in the same military headquarters city of Rawalpindi, half a century earlier, Prime Minister Liaquat Ali Khan had been assassinated. Many feared that Benazir's murder would trigger a return to martial rule, but Musharraf had earlier turned over his baton of military command to General Ashfaq Parvez Kayani, a more cautious younger officer, apparently less tempted to usurp political power.

The PPP rode a tidal wave to victory in 2008. Benazir's nineteen-year-old son, Bilawal, was too young to take up her mantle, however, and he returned to Oxford, leaving his father, Asif Ali Zardari, to serve as chairman of the party. Nawaz Sharif, whose Muslim League–Nawaz Party won the second largest block of seats in Islamabad's Assembly, initially agreed to allow several of his party's members to join a PPP-led coalition cabinet in Islamabad. But Nawaz swiftly lost faith in Zardari, who refused to agree to reappoint Iftikhar Chaudhry as chief justice of the Supreme Court, despite his "firm" preelection commitment to do so. Nawaz suspected that Zardari feared that Chaudhry would resurrect charges of corruption against him, possibly even one for the "murder" of Benazir's brother, which had been dropped by Musharraf when he and Benazir agreed to share power. Nawaz was also eager to charge Musharraf himself with high treason for launching his coup against him when he was Pakistan's elected prime minister. Zardari's refusal to agree to Nawaz's demands drove him out of their tenuous coalition, leaving Benazir's widower to run for president himself in September. Though without Nawaz's support, Zardari won the election, in great measure a sympathy vote to console him for his wife's death. Thus President Zardari, long reviled as "Mr. 10 Percent" because of his reputed demand for a cut of every official deal while his wife was prime minister, moved into the palace vacated by Musharraf on 7 September 2008.

Nawaz now led the opposition in Islamabad's Assembly and controlled Punjab, in which his brother Shahbaz Sharif returned to his former job as chief minister in Lahore. Zardari chose Yousaf Raza Gilani, an obscure young PPP loyalist, to serve as Pakistan's prime minister. Powerful older members of the PPP had little faith in Zardari's judgment. He was, after all, no Bhutto, and Zulfi's closest relatives, including his "brother-uncle" Mumtaz Bhutto, considered Zardari little more than an incompetent "usurper" of power.[1] President Zardari's major source of strength was in Washington, where some believed he was more pro-Western than Nawaz, whom they feared to be strongly supportive of Taliban terrorists. Nawaz himself, however, always denied this. He had been forced to leave the coalition "we joined for the restoration of democracy," Nawaz informed the press, because Zardari's early promises to him "were not honored."

Responding to pressure from Washington, Zardari initially urged General Kayani to do whatever was necessary to take back Pakistan's beautiful Swat Valley, only 100 miles north of Islamabad, from the Taliban, into whose hands it had fallen during the previous year. Swat and Bajaur were being turned into "hell" by the followers of the Taliban mullah Fakir Mohammed and

Maulana Fazlullah, who hanged innocent civilians, burned girls' schools to the ground, and whipped young women who dared to walk outside alone without covering themselves in black, forcing tens of thousands to flee their terror. The Red Cross called the region "a war zone."

On 20 September 2008, the best-protected part of Islamabad also fell victim, as a bomb-filled old truck was driven up to the very entrance of its posh, heavily guarded Marriott Hotel, blowing a hole in the ground twenty feet deep, killing fifty-four innocents, wounding hundreds of others, and almost eliminating Pakistan's entire cabinet, which had been scheduled to dine there on the eve of Zardari's flight to Washington. Terrified by such displays of Taliban power, Zardari capitulated to their demands a few months later, surrendering the Swat Valley to Taliban leaders, whose newly imposed Sharia law drove hundreds of thousands of its most enlightened residents to abandon their ancestral homes. Baitullah Mehsud, the most feared leader of Pakistan's Taliban, vowed to bring his suicide brand of terror to New York and London, and in March 2009, his followers hit Lahore's Police Academy, killing eight of its new recruits and their trainers. But on 5 August 2009, an unmanned U.S. drone aircraft killed Mehsud and his wife in southern Waziristan.

In September 2008, President Zardari flew to New York to meet with Prime Minister Manmohan Singh at the opening session of the United Nations. They vowed to repair "bridges of friendship" between India and Pakistan and to carry forward the "dialogue peace process" launched in 2004. After that cordial greeting they issued a joint statement, wisely insisting that "hostility and terrorism have no place in the vision they share of the bilateral relationship and . . . severe action would be taken against any elements directing or involved in terrorist acts."[2] They agreed to open the Line of Control in Kashmir to Indo-Pakistani trade starting on 21 October 2008. This New York summit proved so hopeful that some believed it might lead to an early and enduring resolution of all outstanding Indo-Pakistani conflicts, including Kashmir.

On 26 November 2008, however, ten Pakistani terrorists, who had left Karachi by sea, launched three days and nights of suicidal murders in Mumbai, killing at least 173, among them several Jews and Parsis, though most were Hindus. Thanks to India's patient restraint, this despicable attack on its richest city did not escalate into nuclear war, though Pakistan continued to drag its heels with regard to India's demand that it punish the Lashkar terrorist leaders appropriately. Moreover, President Zardari's civil government and General Kayani's army failed lamentably to protect foreign visitors as vital to Pakistan's global status and economy as Sri Lanka's cricket team, whose bus was attacked by twelve motorcycle terrorists on 3 March 2009 in the heart of Lahore, which had been stripped of police despite ample notice of the cricket team's imminent arrival there and solemn promises of protection. Small wonder that no foreign team plans in the foreseeable future to visit Pakistan, which has long prided itself on its cricket diplomacy, as Musharraf called a recent visit by Pakistan's team to Agra in India, where he accompanied them. What must it take for Pakistan's leaders to awaken to the importance of cleansing their own cities of terrorists and inculcating civilized values, which start with the sanctity of life and include proper protection of one's neighbors and guests as well as Pakistan's own citizens?

Pakistan's president had also still to learn that political opponents should never be banned from contesting elections, but can only be beaten democratically: by winning more popular support than they do, from those who should always "run" every free country—its people. Early in 2009, Zardari misguidedly tried to ban Nawaz Sharif and his brother Shahbaz from running for any political offices in the future, and also reaffirmed the illicit firing of Chief Justice Chaudhry. Nawaz refused to be intimidated, however, leading the start of a second great lawyers' march in defiance of Zardari's autocratic orders and continued failure to reappoint Chaudhry to his Supreme Court seat. Calling on all Pakistanis to "rise and revolt," Nawaz swiftly emerged as Pakistan's most popular leader, Zardari sinking to his lowest level in every poll. Shouts for Zardari to "Go!" were almost as loud as those which had led to Musharraf's fall the year before.

Prime Minister Gilani then happily announced on 16 March 2009 that the president's ruling had been rescinded, and Chief Justice Chaudhry was reappointed the same day. Whether Nawaz would return to his former post as prime minister or replace Zardari as president was as yet unclear, though he is the most powerful and popular politician in Pakistan and is likely to remain so for the foreseeable future. Two of the PPP's popular liberal leaders, Barrister Aitzaz Ahsan and Benazir Bhutto's London friend Sherry Rehman, who had quit Zardari's cabinet when he acted so dictatorially, might well join Nawaz in putting together a national coalition, which should have the support of Washington's new Democratic administration as well as Pakistan's popular majority. Meanwhile, Nawaz's brother Shahbaz Sharif reclaimed his former position in Lahore as Punjab's chief minister.

Chief Justice Chaudhry wasted no time in reassuming his role as Pakistan's foremost guardian of civil rights and justice for women as well as men. The brutality of Taliban terrorists in Swat, who had whipped a seventeen-year-old girl for appearing in public without a burka, was properly criticized by the Supreme Court's leader, who soundly reprimanded Pakistan's attorney general for ignoring such crimes instead of arresting their perpetrators. The chief justice, moreover, appointed a special panel to investigate ex-President Musharraf's possible high crimes and ordered Musharraf not to leave Pakistan pending a criminal trial, which was demanded by most of Pakistan's senators, led by Mian Raza Rabbani and Ilyas Bilour, who called him a "thief" and "dacoit."[3] Musharraf had flown off by then to London, however, and may opt never to return to stand trial. However, it now seems at least clear that the judicious spirit of Pakistan's founding father, Jinnah, has been revitalized by the brave chief justice of its Supreme Court. India and the United States should take hope from this encouraging rebirth of the liberal humanitarian rule of law emanating from Pakistan's capital, silenced for too many years by harsh repression.

India's elections in 2004 brought the Congress-led United Progressive Alliance back to power. Prime Minister Manmohan Singh, thanks to whose wisdom India's newly opened economy has enjoyed its miracle of globalized growth since 1991, affirmed his faith in and support of the cease-fire and the comprehensive peace process his predecessor had launched. India's traditional focus on higher education and its faith in science and the humanities has produced a vast pool of well-trained scientists and English-speaking graduates, tens of thousands of whom have over the past few decades been employed in newly built outsourcing centers of information in and around Bangalore and Mumbai, Chennai and New Delhi, linked round the clock to New York, Washington, Boston, and Los Angeles, providing assistance through cyberspace to millions of Americans in coping with their airline reservations, computers, new cars, and electronic machines that break down. The new Indo-U.S. Civil Nuclear Accord has added a strategic partnership to the burgeoning business union between the world's oldest and largest democracies. So while Pakistan sadly sank deeper into civil conflict, India and the United States forged a fresh alliance, sharing intelligence information as well as their most advanced scientific technology.

India's greatest potential internal weakness, however, lies in deep-rooted fears and prejudices against Muslims that many Hindu-first extremists continue to nurture, primarily in wealthy Gujarat, ironically the state in which Mahatma Gandhi was born. Orthodox Hindus believe that their divine king Raja Rama was born at Ayodhya in Uttar Pradesh (UP), at the very site of a Mughal mosque built in the sixteenth century to commemorate the conquest of northern India by Babur, founder of the Mughal Empire. Hindutva organizations led by the Vishwa Hindu Parishad (Universal Hindu Society) launched a national campaign to tear down Babur's mosque (Babri Masjid) and replace it with a reconstruction of "Rama's Birth-temple" *(Ram Janma-bhoomi)*, which they insisted had originally been erected on that very spot. The BJP joined the movement, leading a hundred thousand Hindus to Ayodhya in December 1992, where they used steel rods and brickbats to batter down the old mosque in nine hours of frenzied hammering and loud chanting of Lord Rama's name— "Ram, Ram, Hari!" Police watched unmoving as the mosque, which had withstood the rains of 460 monsoons, crumbled to dust in a day. Shockwaves of communal fury spread across South Asia, leaving thousands dead and hundreds of Hindu temples in Pakistan and Bangladesh pulverized. India's High Court blocked the erection of a new temple on the mosque's old platform, and

Indian troops were stationed around the desecrated area to prevent any further provocation to violence.

A decade later, Hindutva leaders vowed to erect Rama's new birth-temple at the old mosque's site, on 15 March 2002, celebrated as Rama's birthday. Hindu craftsmen had been working without pay for ten years to carve out and polish every stone and marble statue of the new temple, and all those parts were carefully arranged around the site. Fearing violence, however, Prime Minister Vajpayee and Deputy Prime Minister L. K. Advani deployed 15,000 of India's best riot-control police in Ayodhya shortly before the birth celebration began. Many Hindu workers lost heart then and decided to return home, leaving Ayodhya on the Sabarmati Express in late February, stopping at Godhra station. There a few Hindus stepped down for tea, bumping into a mad Muslim railwayman. He cursed them and threw a flaming torch through the window of their carriage. Other Muslims joined in, trapping fifty-six Hindu men, women, and children, all of whom were burned to death inside the blazing steel coach.

The aftermath proved even worse. As the news spread across Gujarat, thousands of Hindutva thugs raced after any Muslims they could find, setting fire to their beards and turbans and beating them to death if they had not burned to death first. Gujarat's BJP chief minister, Narendra Modi, did nothing to stop the massacre, leaving more than two thousand Muslims to be slaughtered in the next few days before the fires of Hindu rage abated. Modi gave no orders to arrest or prosecute any of the murderers, remarking to Hindu colleagues in provincial power that "Jinnah was right! Muslims should all leave India and go to Pakistan!" Modi was reelected that year with his largest majority and soon became the political hero of every reactionary Hindu group in India and many wealthy overseas friends of the BJP, who tout him as their favorite future candidate for prime minister. Most Indians proved more sensible, however, and elected the liberal secular Congress party and its progressive allies in 2004. This United Progressive Alliance coalition not only prevailed again in the 2009 national elections, but the Congress party itself almost doubled its lead over the BJP, nearly winning a Lok Sabha majority on its own. Dr. Farooq Abdullah of Kashmir, moreover, was brought into Prime Minister Singh's Cabinet as its minister for new and renewable energy, while his son, Omar Abdullah, was elected to lead Srinagar's state assembly as its chief minister, bolstering the power of Jammu and Kashmir state's relations with the central government.

Free elections were held in Jammu and Kashmir in 2005 for the first time in years, when violence in the Vale of Kashmir briefly declined as the regularly scheduled Peace Bus started to cross the Line of Control that April between Srinagar and Muzaffarabad. But that spring thaw did not last long, suicide bombings increasing as soon as Kashmiris began to hope for permanent reconciliation among their diverse parties. Every market and crowded theater, any bus terminal or train station, became a target for terrorists, who had nothing better to live for, it seemed, than random acts of violence and killing innocents. How could so many young men find death linked to murder more inviting and appealing than the infinitely wondrous prospects of life itself?

In June 2008, Kashmir erupted again when the Congress-led provincial government transferred ninety-nine acres of empty land to the Amarnath Shrine Board, run by Hindus, to be used for building rest houses and medical stations for the thousands of Hindu pilgrims who annually trekked an arduous twenty-six miles to the icicle cave of Amarnath, where Hindus believe Lord

Shiva lives inside the mountain. This *yatra* (pilgrimage trek) often proved fatal to elderly devotees, and the idea of erecting rest houses on the unused land seemed to state leaders both sensible and humane. But protests flared in every quarter of Srinagar as news of the "giveaway" of property to "attract" more Hindu tourists to Kashmir spread, triggering mass outcries of "Azaadi!" Troops shot and killed several of the most militant Muslims, injuring hundreds more, as Kashmir's Hurriyat Conference led marches of up to 100,000 shouting protesters through Srinagar's streets, demanding that Indian troops be withdrawn once and for all from the Vale.

Then the state government changed its mind, taking back the gift of land from the Hindu Shrine Board, triggering protests throughout Jammu against Kashmir's "spineless" administration. Hindutva BJP activists nationwide hoped to benefit in the 2009 elections from what Narendra Modi called the "betrayal of all Hindus" by Kashmir's "cowardly" state government. Hurriyat leader Shahid-ul-Islam urged Kashmiri protesters to remain calm and prove that Kashmiri Muslims were determined to win their freedom peacefully from India's "terrorist" Hindu troops. Another, more militant Hurriyat leader, Sheikh Abdul Aziz, was shot dead by an officer as he cried aloud for "Azaadi!"

UN Secretary-General Ban Ki-moon has recently insisted that "the Kashmir question . . . of nearly six decades will not go away and an effort is urgently required to resolve it."[4] The question that remains, however, is just how best to achieve that still singularly elusive resolution.

TEN

Potential Solutions
to the Kashmir Conflict

A permanent peaceful resolution to Kashmir's conflict will require solemn diplomatic agreements between India and Pakistan that have the full support of Kashmir's most popular leaders. For ten years after the Kashmir problem was first brought to the UN Security Council by India, heroic efforts were made by the UNCIP's global diplomats to resolve the conflict through a comprehensive or limited plebiscite supervised by UN monitors, or by the division of Jammu and Kashmir into its dominant ethno-religious units—Hindu Jammu and Buddhist Ladakh going to India, and the Muslim-majority Kashmir Valley to Pakistan.

India's repeated adamant refusal to accept any of those Security Council proposed resolutions, however, has by now removed them from the realm of realistic options. The Simla Accord of 1972, which committed both India and Pakistan to settling "their differences by peaceful means through bilateral negotiations," explicitly ruled out any "unilateral altering" of the situation, or multinational resolutions of the conflict, keeping the United States out of any open mediatory role in creating a final resolution for Kashmir. In 2004, both Vajpayee and Musharraf appeared ready, nonetheless, to agree on a "last try" to resolve this toughest of current global conflicts by accepting the Line of Control as the Indo-Pakistani international border. Musharraf then immediately reneged, however, insisting that he could never agree to thus seeking to turn the "cause" of their conflict over Kashmir into its resolution. His Punjabi military colleagues had apparently refused to consider Vajpayee's final solution in any way acceptable.

National independent statehood for Kashmir has also often been mooted over the past sixty years, initially by the maharajah of Kashmir himself, and most recently by a number of young Azaadis in Srinagar, but that proposal has never won any official support from either India or Pakistan, without which it remains an implausible option.

The most realistic solution to the Kashmir conflict, therefore, would appear to be acceptance of the current Line of Control that now divides the former princely state of Jammu and Kashmir as the northernmost international border of India and Pakistan. Though many Pakistanis still favor reunification of the Vale of Kashmir and its integration into Pakistan, based on the tested preferences of its majority, Pakistan's tragic failure to sustain a freely elected civil polity capable of protecting its own people for long, whatever their gender or faith might be, has reduced virtually to zero the credibility of its repeated demands for self-determination for Kashmir's Muslim majority. Until Pakistan's elected leaders are strong enough to control the Al-Qaeda and Taliban militants who inhabit its entire Afghan frontier, and to end the nurturing on

Pakistani soil of suicide bombers bent on killing Indians, Americans, Sri Lankans, or other innocent people the world over, their demands for a democratic resolution of Kashmir's conflict will have little credibility and win scant support.

To suggest, however, that the most feasible solution to the Kashmir conflict should be to accept the status quo of the current territorial division of the Vale of Kashmir is not to argue that India should continue its military occupation and praetorian attacks on Kashmir's Muslim majority. The people of Kashmir themselves must be permitted to choose their own leaders in free and fair elections, as do Indians in every other state in that union, and New Delhi should solemnly commit to supporting Kashmir's provincial autonomy and the human rights of its people, as it does the autonomy and rights of the people of Punjab, Maharashtra, or West Bengal. India's present United Progressive Alliance should have no difficulty endorsing so humane an agreement, since, as Prime Minister Manmohan Singh said when launching the first Kashmir train service on 11 October 2008: "We must create conditions whereby a Kashmiri living in Srinagar or Muzaffarabad should not see any problem about people-to-people contacts." He then wisely welcomed better relations with Pakistan as "essential" to India's "best" interests. Ten days later the Line of Control was opened for the first time in sixty years to civil trade between Srinagar and Muzaffarabad, though that traffic in the reverse direction proved less promising in its first months at least, some of the produce to India from Pakistan either being looted before it could leave or contaminated by the time it arrived.

The most troubling potential obstacle to the viability of this Kashmir solution is the possibility of the election in India of another BJP-led central government in the foreseeable future, especially were it dominated by anti-Muslim Hindutva extremists like Narendra Modi. This hypothetical possibility would dangerously diminish the prospects of permanent Indo-Pakistani peace, without which no solution for Kashmir is possible. Hopefully, the majority of India's electorate will, however, continue to prefer progressively tolerant leaders rather than narrowly bigoted ones, peacemakers rather than warmongers, choosing a bright and promising future rather than reverting to ancient, deadly religious conflicts. Pakistan, of course, must also firmly establish a democratic civil government capable of maintaining the support and respect of its military leaders in subduing Islamic militants and Taliban extremists.

"If the leaders of Pakistan have the courage, the determination and the statesmanship to take this road to peace," Prime Minister Singh encouraged them on 9 June 2009, "I wish to assure them that we will meet them more than half way."[1] A month later, accepting an honorary doctorate from Jammu University, Manmohan Singh reiterated the theme of peace, saying, "I hope and believe that Jammu and Kashmir can, one day, become a symbol of India-Pakistan cooperation rather than of conflict. . . . Borders cannot be changed, but they can be made irrelevant . . . the Line of Control can become a line of peace with a free flow of ideas, goods, services and people."[2]

The 10th International Kashmir Peace Conference, held in Washington, D.C., on 23–24 July 2009, under the auspices of the Kashmiri American Council, led by Dr. Ghulam Nabi Fai, and the Association of Humanitarian Lawyers USA, led by Dr. Karen Parker, unanimously urged "the cessation of militarization and human rights violations" throughout Kashmir.[3] The Kashmir Peace Conference received and heard messages from all top Kashmir leaders, including those detained in jails—Syed Ali Geelani and Shabir Ahmed Shah—and from those under house arrest, including Mirwaiz Umar Farooq and Muhammad Yasin Malik. These courageous Kashmiri leaders "called upon the global leadership to impress on the Government of India" the urgent need "to end its reign of terror in Kashmir, release all political prisoners and play a pro-active role in the resolution of the sixty-two-year-old Kashmir problem."[4]

In May 2009, accusations were made that two young Kashmiri women had been raped and murdered by Indian police or soldiers, who were charged with those crimes by the International People's Tribunal on Human Rights and Justice in Indian-administered Kashmir. That tribunal's report was presented to the 10th International Kashmir Peace Conference by Dr. Angana Chatterji. "A will to peace in Kashmir requires an attested commitment to justice, palpably absent in the exchanges undertaken by the Government of India and its attendant institutions with Kashmir civil society," she read. "The . . . structure of impunity connected to militarization, and corresponding human rights abuses, bear witness to the absence of accountability inherent to the dominion of Kashmir by the Indian state."[5] Months of violent protests shut down the town of Shopian, thirty-five miles south of Srinagar, where the girls' dead bodies were found in the usually shallow Rambi River. Autopsies by Kashmiri doctors concluded that the murdered girls had been raped, after which four local police officers were arrested for "suppressing and destroying evidence in the case."[6] Then, on 28 September 2009, a team of New Delhi doctors conducted more elaborate autopsies, including DNA testing by forensic experts from the All India Institute of Medical Science, who studied tissue taken from both corpses, which had been exhumed by India's Central Bureau of Investigation (CBI). The CBI team, which examined the autopsy findings, reported that both girls had died of suffocation caused by drowning. Kashmiri doctors who had performed the first autopsies were then charged with "falsifying evidence . . . to serve an ideological agenda." The four arrested policemen were released. "It is nothing but a bundle of lies," said Shakheel Ahmed Ahangar.[7] His dead wife, Neelofar Jan, had just recently turned twenty-two; her dead sister, Asiya Jan, was only seventeen.

Dr. Fai concluded the Kashmir Peace Conference he chaired by appealing to "the Obama Administration for serious engagement of the United States with both India and Pakistan for a speedy resolution of the festering Kashmir problem."[8] U.S. support will encourage both India and Pakistan to work with Kashmir's leaders in drafting diplomatic agreements to maintain the cease-fire started in 2004, and then progressively to withdraw all their troops from the new international border, the former Line of Control, and all military and paramilitary police from the Vale of Kashmir. India might insist on keeping a token force for several more years in Srinagar itself, but Kashmiris should be trained to maintain their own security, and the establishment of a joint Indo-Pakistani-Kashmiri team of special troops could be established to implement such training, written into the Peace Treaty in its final form. The drawing down of troops might take a bit longer, depending on how well the initial phase progressed, but considering the length of the Kashmir conflict, that would hardly be surprising.

Bilateral Indo-Pakistani agreements specifying greater cooperation economically, educationally, and culturally between New Delhi and Islamabad would also be required as part of this permanent peace process. Kashmiri Hurriyat, Jammu Hindu, and Ladakhi Buddhist leaders should be elected to serve on each of these joint Indo-Pakistani Commissions, contributing their vital local knowledge and vision in all such cooperative areas from the start of the process. The headquarters of each Kashmir peace subcommission could be based permanently in Srinagar, New Delhi, Islamabad, and Muzaffarabad. The permanent secretariat of the SAARC in Kathmandu should support the Kashmir peace process in every possible way, and the UN Security Council should also be part of this international process of constant cooperation and monitoring assistance.

The importance of bolstering Pakistan's economy and strengthening its educational institutions need hardly be elaborated upon, but here again the process of institution-building will prove slow, arduous, and obviously expensive, though in the long run relatively reasonable compared to the cost of continuing the conflict and the threat of nuclear war. The current U.S. commitment of $1.5 billion a year for five years to help Pakistan strengthen its educational system is but a first step in this sensible direction of global support to the peace-building process in South Asia. Arms alone, no matter how modern or powerfully remote, will never solve problems deeply buried in the hearts and minds of hundreds of millions of people. Nor will education alone do the complex job of rebuilding lives and opening minds. Yet with the prospect of productive, challenging, and peaceful jobs at the end of the educational process, Pakistan's citizens will surely soon learn to reject violence and communal hatred, recognizing instead the values and beauty of leading fruitful, peaceful lives.

The creation of a nationwide "Pakistan *Quaid* [Great Leader] Service Corps," modeled on our AmeriCorps, could help reeducate enough young Pakistanis to accelerate the process of change required to transform Pakistan from its current state of sectarian religious preoccupation to a more secular modernity. Most Pakistanis continue to admire their *Quaid-i-Azam* Jinnah, but few realize how secular, liberal, and judicious a man he actually was. The new Service Corps would, therefore, include the reeducation of its volunteers in their own history as well as courses on social welfare, public health, economic development, urban planning, and global cooperation. Each young volunteer could sign on initially for one year, with the option of renewing the contract. My hope is that in the first five years, many thousands of Pakistan's potentially best and brightest future leaders would be enrolled in this *Quaid* Service Corps.

Some Americans, sickened by the murder and mayhem daily reported from Pakistan, believe that all U.S. aid to Pakistan should cease. Many Indians are similarly inclined to believe that the recent plague of terror unleashed by Pakistani extremists puts their entire population beyond rational reach, deserving neither assistance nor compassion. Yet more than 160 million moderate Pakistani Muslims would thus be left to the destructive domination and lack of mercy of at most a few million Taliban and Al-Qaeda terrorists and their sympathizers living along Pakistan's frontier. The result of so unconscionable a policy is too perilous to contemplate. Our world is so tightly linked today that no nation, indeed no island, can long remain isolated, unaffected by or unaffecting all of us. If Pakistan should ever succumb to the madness of its Taliban terrorist minority, or to the allure of Al-Qaeda's extremist form of jihad, all of South Asia might then become victims of that same deadly disease, capable even of spreading globally. For the world to abandon Pakistan today could mean finding ourselves forced to fight nuclear-armed Taliban and Al-Qaeda suicide bombers in the future. That would be tantamount to abandoning civilization as we know it.

"The only thing we have to fear is fear itself," President Franklin D. Roosevelt taught us in March 1933, in his first inaugural address. Taliban bombers have now proved to be their own worst enemies, forcing most Pakistanis to recognize how vital the need to confront and defeat such terrorists is to the very survival of their nation. No alternative exists. In April 2009, two months after the government of Pakistan had surrendered to Taliban demands to give Islam's medieval Sharia law free reign in the Swat Valley, Taliban killers moved into neighboring Buner District to its south, swiftly taking over there as well. Local police were too weak to stop these ideologically motivated, well-armed zealots from closing down every female school and music shop in the district, just seventy miles north of Islamabad itself. Pakistan's army was finally sent down from Peshawar to deal with this fast-moving rebellion aimed at the heart of Pakistan's capital. The army has always been Pakistan's strongest institution, its final arbiter at setting the limits "on what is *possible* in Pakistan."[9] Without its army to protect and defend Pakistanis themselves from the multifaceted threat now posed by Taliban insurgents, nuclear-armed Pakistan would pose, as Secretary of State Hillary Rodham Clinton rightly put it to Congress, "a mortal threat to the security and safety of our country and the world."[10]

On 7 July 2009, President Zardari admitted that Pakistani "militants and extremists" had been "created and nurtured" by Pakistani military trainers for "attacks launched in India" prior to 11 September 2001. It was the first such high-level admission from Islamabad that the charges India's Foreign Ministry had been making for years were true. "India's stand has been vindicated," Foreign Minister S. M. Krishna responded, but now Pakistan must "take action" against those "conspiracies and conspirators."[11] That same day in July, the U.S. Treasury froze all the assets of four Pakistani "terrorists" linked both to Lashkar-e-Tayiba and Al-Qaeda, one of them with connections to Karachi's underworld don Dawood Ibrahim, in planning the Mumbai commuter train bombings of July 2006.[12] Those four newly designated "global terrorists" from Pakistan's Lashkar-e-Tayiba were Arif Qasmani, chief coordinator of the 2008 Mumbai terrorist attack; Fazeel-Ameen al-Peshawari, who provided funds and recruits to Al-Qaeda; Yahya Mujahid, head of the Lashkar's media department since 2001; and Nasir Javaid, commander of the Lashkar's operations and training center in Pakistan. The Muslim mullah who launched the Lashkar in 1989 to train Pakistani terrorists sent across the Line of Control into India, Hafiz M. Saeed, was initially placed under house arrest in Pakistan soon after the 2008 Mumbai attacks had ended, but a few months later was released by order of Pakistan's High Court of Lahore, which insisted that there was "insufficient evidence" to hold him. Nonetheless, the Pakistani authorities handed over their intelligence file on the Lashkar's terrorist funding and training to India's government in mid-July 2009. Pakistan is finally preparing to try five Lashkar operatives recently arrested in Karachi for planning the Mumbai attack, including its "mastermind," Zaki-ur-Rehman Lakhvi, who issued cell-phone orders to his killers in Mumbai from his base in Karachi, reminding them that they "must not be taken alive."

On 20 July 2009, the only Pakistani terrorist invader of Mumbai taken alive, Ajmal Amir Kasab, startled the High Court in which he was being tried for murder by confessing "to all my crimes."[13] Kasab had not even told his lawyer of his intention to confess. He then informed Judge M. L. Tahiliyani that he and his fellow Lashkar terrorists had all been "trained" for a month and a half in a "safe house" in Karachi before setting sail for Mumbai.

After landing in Mumbai, Kasab and his partner, Abu Ismail, attacked the central railway terminal, firing their automatic rifles indiscriminately and hurling their hand grenades, killing 52 people and wounding 109 more. They then moved on to wreak havoc at Cama Hospital. Kasab named four Lashkar "persons" who had prepared the terrorist team of ten for their hideous job, seeing them off at Karachi's port: "Zaki-ur Rehman Lakhvi, Abu Hamza, Abu Kafa, and Abu Jundala."[14] Little more than one year after his trial had begun, Kasab was found guilty of "waging war against India," and on 8 May 2010 he was sentenced to death by hanging.

Pakistan's imminent trials of its Lashkar leaders, charged with planning and funding the brutal attacks in Mumbai and against India's embassy in Kabul, where 54 Indians and Afghan employees were killed earlier, should be open to India's press and transparent in procedure, providing the "visible response" to Pakistani terrorist actions that New Delhi has long demanded. As India's Foreign Secretary Shivshankar Menon told his Pakistani counterpart, Salman Bashir, during their mid-July 2009 Non-Aligned Movement (NAM) meeting at Sharm-el-Sheikh: "Pakistan should give us an undertaking that they will not let their soil be used for terrorist activities directed against India."[15] The next day, Pakistan's Prime Minister Gilani personally promised India's Prime Minister Singh that Islamabad was ready to cooperate fully with India in ending future terrorist attacks designed to provoke hatred and incite possible war with India. If Pakistan's civil leadership has the strength and courage firmly to enforce Gilani's promise, then India's wisdom in resisting all demands from its own militants to respond more forcefully to the Mumbai attack will have been fully vindicated. Such brave cooperation in tackling terrorist provocations and rejecting violent retaliatory responses is the most encouraging step by India and Pakistan on the high road to peace for South Asia. Just one day after that summit meeting at Sharm-el-Sheikh promising India's peaceful cooperation with Pakistan, however, the entire BJP-led opposition angrily stormed out of Parliament, accusing Prime Minister Singh of "betraying" his promise that "there would be no talks with Pakistan" until the latter fully admitted its role in launching terrorist attacks against India and had properly "punished" those terrorists.[16]

Many angry and frustrated extremists in both nations will, doubtless, try to derail the peace process. It might require years, if not decades, of patience and persistent fortitude before India and Pakistan finally attain sanity and prosperity together. But the younger generations of both nations will surely prevail, should their elders lose heart and seek to fall back upon ancient religious hatreds or narrow national antipathies.

The music of peace played by Salman Ahmad's great rock band Junoon is as popular today among the youth of India as in its birthplace in Pakistan. Mira Nair's brilliant films bring joy and tears to the hearts and eyes of as many young Pakistani devotees as they do to their millions of ardent fans throughout India. And Arundhati Roy's novel *The God of Small Things* has inspired readers throughout the world, as have her subsequent courageous essays defying electrified fences and high concrete walls erected to divide people, but incapable of screening out joyous songs of love and freedom, and our universal longing for peace.

NOTES

INTRODUCTION

1. See Stanley Wolpert, *Shameful Flight: The Last Years of the British Empire in India* (New York: Oxford University Press, 2006).

ONE. THE HISTORIC ROOTS OF THE PROBLEM

1. Nehru's inaugural address as prime minister on 14 August 1947 was titled "Tryst with Destiny." See Stanley Wolpert, *Nehru: A Tryst with Destiny* (New York: Oxford University Press, 1996).

2. Stanley Wolpert, *Tilak and Gokhale: Revolution and Reform in the Making of Modern India* (Berkeley: University of California Press, 1962); Stanley Wolpert, *Morley and India, 1906–1910* (Berkeley: University of California Press, 1967).

3. Stanley Wolpert, *Jinnah of Pakistan* (New York: Oxford University Press, 1984).

4. Wolpert, *Shameful Flight*, pp. 129–30.

5. Ibid., pp. 166–69. For a more complete discussion of the Punjab border changes, see Robert G. Wirsing, *India, Pakistan, and the Kashmir Dispute* (New York: St. Martin's Press, 1994), pp. 12–34. W. H. Auden captured the futility of Radcliffe's labors in his poem "Partition."

6. Wolpert, *Shameful Flight*, p. 192. See also Rajmohan Gandhi, *Revenge & Reconciliation: Understanding South Asian History* (New Delhi: Penguin Books, 1999).

TWO. THE FIRST INDO-PAKISTANI WAR

1. *Kalhaṇa's "Rājataraṅginī": A Chronicle of the Kings of Kaśmīr*, trans. and ed. Marc Aurel Stein (Westminster, UK: A. Constable, 1900).

2. Josef Korbel, *Danger in Kashmir* (Princeton: Princeton University Press, 1954), passim.

3. See Wirsing, *India, Pakistan, and the Kashmir Dispute*.

THREE. THE SECOND INDO-PAKISTANI WAR

1. Mohammad Ayub Khan, *Friends Not Masters: A Political Autobiography* (New York: Oxford University Press, 1967).

2. Stanley Wolpert, *Zulfi Bhutto of Pakistan* (New York: Oxford University Press, 1993).

3. Sumit Ganguly, *The Crisis in Kashmir: Portents of War, Hopes of Peace* (Washington, DC: Woodrow Wilson Center Press; New York: Cambridge University Press, 1997), p. 46.

4. C. P. Srivastava, *Lal Bahadur Shastri* (Delhi: Oxford University Press, 1995), p. 353.

5. Wolpert, *Zulfi Bhutto*, p. 102.

FOUR. THE THIRD INDO-PAKISTANI WAR AND THE BIRTH OF BANGLADESH

1. Wolpert, *Jinnah of Pakistan*, pp. 184–85. Emphasis added.

2. The best work on this war is Richard Sisson and Leo Rose, *War and Secession: Pakistan, India, and the Creation of Bangladesh* (Berkeley: University of California Press, 1990).

FIVE. FROM THE SIMLA SUMMIT TO ZIA'S COUP

1. Piloo Mody, *Zulfi, My Friend* (Delhi: Thomson Press, 1973), p. 141.

2. "The Simla Agreement" is published in Ganguly, *Crisis in Kashmir*, as appendix 4, pp. 166–68.

3. *Dr. A. Q. Khan on Pakistan Bomb*, ed. Sreedar (New Delhi: ABC Publishing House, 1987), pp. 43–44.

4. George Percovich, *India's Nuclear Bomb: The Impact on Global Proliferation* (Berkeley: University of California Press, 1999).

5. Wolpert, *Zulfi Bhutto of Pakistan*, p. 327.

SIX. AFGHANISTAN'S IMPACT
ON INDO-PAKISTANI RELATIONS

1. Stanley Wolpert, *Roots of Confrontation in South Asia: Afghanistan, Pakistan, India and the Superpowers* (New York: Oxford University Press, 1982). Narendra Singh Sarila, *The Shadow of the Great Game: The Untold Story of India's Partition* (New York: Carroll & Graf, 2005).

2. Wolpert, *Roots of Confrontation*, p. 55.

3. Wirsing, *India, Pakistan, and the Kashmir Dispute*, pp. 195–216.

4. Benazir Bhutto, *Reconciliation: Islam, Democracy, and the West* (New York: HarperCollins, 2008), p. 199.

5. Ahmed Rashid, *Taliban: Militant Islam, Oil and Fundamentalism in Central Asia* (New Haven: Yale University Press, 2000).

SEVEN. PAKISTAN'S PROXY WAR
AND KASHMIR'S *AZAADI* REVOLUTION

1. Sumantra Bose, *Kashmir: Roots of Conflict, Paths to Peace* (Cambridge, MA: Harvard University Press, 2003), p. 93.

2. Navnita Chadha Behera, *Demystifying Kashmir* (Washington, DC: Brookings Institution, 2006), p. 48.

3. Ajit Bhattacharjea, *Kashmir: The Wounded Valley* (New Delhi: UBS Publishers, 1994).

EIGHT. RECENT ATTEMPTS TO RESOLVE THE ESCALATING CONFLICT

1. Stephen P. Cohen, "Why Did India 'Go Nuclear'?" in *India's Nuclear Security*, ed. Raju G. C. Thomas and Amit Gupta (Boulder, CO: Lynne Rienner, 2000), pp. 13–35.

2. Farah Zarah, "Pakistan's Elusive Search for Nuclear Parity with India," in *India's Nuclear Security*, ed. Thomas and Gupta, pp. 145–70.

3. "Indian and Pakistani Weapons," chap. 3 in Scott D. Sagan and Kenneth N. Waltz, *The Spread of Nuclear Weapons: A Debate Renewed, with New Sections on India and Pakistan, Terrorism, and Missile Defense* (New York: Norton, 2003), pp. 88–108.

4. Pervez Musharraf, *In the Line of Fire: A Memoir* (New York: Free Press, 2006), pp. 120–34.

5. Strobe Talbott, *Engaging India: Diplomacy, Democracy, and the Bomb* (Washington, DC: Brookings Institution, 2004), pp. 174–75.

6. See Kanti P. Bajpai et al., *Brasstacks and Beyond: Perception and Management of Crisis in South Asia* (New Delhi: Manohar, 1995), pp. 1–67.

7. General Krishnaswamy Sundarji, *Blind Men of Hindoostan: Indo-Pak Nuclear War* (New Delhi: UBS, 1993), p. xvi.

8. Ahmed Rashid, *Descent into Chaos: How the War against Islamic Extremism Is Being Lost in Pakistan, Afghanistan and Central Asia* (London: Allen Lane, 2007).

9. Musharraf, *In the Line of Fire*, p. 209.

10. Wolpert, *Jinnah of Pakistan*, p. 337.

NINE. THE STALLED PEACE PROCESS

1. Sardar Mumtaz Ali Bhutto, "I Told You So," an article "banned . . . by the Zardari government . . . ," e-mailed to the author from Karachi on 1 April 2009.

2. Somini Sengupta, "India and Pakistan Open Kashmir Trade Point," *New York Times*, 22 October 2008, p. A10.

3. *Pakistan Link* (Islamabad), 31 July 2009, p. P9.

4. Rediff India Abroad, 12 January 2007; GeoTV, 15 February 2009.

TEN. POTENTIAL SOLUTIONS
TO THE KASHMIR CONFLICT

1. Manmohan Singh quoted in Matthias Williams's article in *India Journal* (Los Angeles), 12 June 2009, p. A33.

2. Press Trust of India, report from Jammu University, 15 July 2009, in *India Journal*, 20 July 2009, p. A24.

3. Washington Declaration text e-mailed to the author by Dr. Ghulam Nabi Fai, 24 July 2009.

4. Kashmir American Council, e-mail to the author, 27 July 2009.

5. "Militarization with Impunity," report of the International People's Tribunal on Human Rights and Justice in Indian-Administered Kashmir (IPTK), presented to the 10th International Kashmir Peace Conference by Dr. Angana Chatterji, 23–24 July 2009.

6. Aijaz Hussain, Associated Press, *IndiaWest* (San Leandro, CA), 2 October 2009, p. A36.

7. Lydia Polgreen, "Women's Deaths, and Inquiry Findings, Enrage Kashmir," *New York Times*, 25 December 2009, p. A4.

8. Dr. Ghulam Nabi Fai, e-mail to the author from Washington, DC, 27 July 2009.

9. Stephen Philip Cohen, *The Idea of Pakistan* (Washington, DC: Brookings Institution, 2004), pp. 97–130.

10. *New York Times*, 23 April 2009, p. A13.

11. Press Trust of India, New Delhi report, *IndiaWest* (San Leandro, CA), 17 July 2009, p. A38.

12. Press Trust of India, Washington report, *IndiaWest* (San Leandro, CA), 17 July 2009, p. A32.

13. Alex Rodriguez and Anshul Rana, "Mumbai Gunman Confesses to Deadly Attacks," *Los Angeles Times*, 21 July 2009, p. A14.

14. From Kasab's "Confession in Court," 20 July 2009, by Kartikeya, *IndiaWest* (San Leandro, CA), 24 July 2009, p. A37.

15. Press Trust of India, Sharm-el-Sheikh report, 14 July 2009, *India Journal*, 17 July 2009, p. A26.

16. Muneeza Naqvi, Associated Press report, *IndiaWest* (San Leandro, CA), 24 July 2009, p. A35.

SELECT BIBLIOGRAPHY

Abbas, K. Ahmed. *Kashmir Fights for Freedom*. Bombay: Kutub, 1948.

Abdullah, Farooq. *My Dismissal*. New Delhi: Vikas, 1985.

Abdullah, Sheikh M. *Flames of the Chinar: An Autobiography*. Trans. Khushwant Singh. New Delhi: Viking, 1993.

Ahmad, Ishtaq. *Gulbuddin Hekmatyar: An Afghan Trail from Jihad to Terrorism*. Lahore: Society for Tolerance, 2004.

Akbar, M.J. *Kashmir: Behind the Vale*. New Delhi: Viking, 1991.

Akhtar, Shaheen. *Uprising in Indian-Held Jammu and Kashmir*. Islamabad: Institute of Regional Studies, 1991.

Amnesty International. *India: Torture and Deaths in Custody in Jammu and Kashmir*. New York: Amnesty International USA, 1995.

Asia Watch. *Human Rights in India: Kashmir under Siege*. New York: Human Rights Watch, 1991.

———. *The Human Rights Crisis in Kashmir: A Pattern of Impunity*. Rawalpindi: Kashmir Press International; New York: Human Rights Watch, 1993.

Bajpai, Kanti P., et al. *Brasstacks and Beyond: Perception and Management of Crisis in South Asia*. New Delhi: Manohar, 1995.

Bamzai, Prithvi Nath Kaul. *A History of Kashmir: Political, Social, Cultural—From the Earliest Times to the Present Day*. Delhi: Metropolitan, 1962.

Bazaz, Prem Nath. *The History of Struggle for Freedom in Kashmir: Cultural and Political*. New Delhi: Kashmir Publishing Company, 1954.

Behera, Navnita Chadha. *Demystifying Kashmir*. Washington, DC: Brookings Institution, 2006.

Bhattacharjea, Ajit. *Kashmir: The Wounded Valley*. New Delhi: UBSPD, 1994.

Bhutto, Benazir. *Reconciliation: Islam, Democracy, and the West*. New York: HarperCollins, 2008.

Bokhari, I.H., and T.P. Thornton. *The 1972 Simla Agreement: An Asymmetrical Negotiation*. Washington, DC: Johns Hopkins School of Advanced International Studies, 1988.

Bose, Sumantra. *Kashmir: Roots of Conflict, Paths to Peace*. Cambridge, MA: Harvard University Press, 2003.

Brines, Russell. *The Indo-Pakistani Conflict*. London: Pall Mall, 1968.

Brown, W. Norman. *The United States and India and Pakistan*. Cambridge: Harvard University Press, 1963.

Chengappa, Raj. *Weapons of Peace: The Secret Story of India's Quest to Be a Nuclear Power*. New Delhi: HarperCollins, 2000.

Cohen, Stephen Philip. *The Idea of Pakistan*. Washington, DC: Brookings Institution, 2004.

———, ed. *The Security of South Asia: American and Asian Perspectives*. Urbana: University of Illinois Press, 1987.

Dasgupta, Chandrashekhar. *War and Diplomacy in Kashmir, 1947–48*. New Delhi; Thousand Oaks, CA: Sage, 2002.

Das Gupta, Jyoti Bhusan. *Jammu and Kashmir*. The Hague: Martinus Nijhoff, 1968.

Engineer, Ashgar Ali. *Secular Crown on Fire: The Kashmir Problem*. Delhi: Ajanta, 1991.

Facets of a Proxy War. New Delhi: Government of India, 1993.

Ganai, A.J. *Kashmir National Conference and History and Politics, 1975–1980*. Srinagar: Gulshan, 1984.

Gandhi, Rajmohan. *Revenge & Reconciliation: Understanding South Asian History*. New Delhi: Penguin Books, 1999.

Ganguly, Sumit. *The Origins of War in South Asia: Indo-Pakistani Conflicts since 1947*. 1986. 2nd ed. Boulder, CO: Westview Press, 1994.

———. *The Crisis in Kashmir: Portents of War, Hopes for Peace*. Washington, DC: Woodrow Wilson Center; New York: Cambridge University Press, 1997.

Gundevia, Y. D. *Outside the Archives*. Hyderabad: Sangam Books, 1984.

Gupta, Sisir. *Kashmir: A Study in India—Pakistan Relations*. Bombay: Asia House, 1966.

Jagmohan. *My Frozen Turbulence in Kashmir*. New Delhi: Allied Publishers, 1991.

Jha, Prem Shankar. *Kashmir, 1947: Rival Versions of History*. Delhi: Oxford University Press, 1996.

Kadian, Rajesh. *The Kashmir Tangle: Issues and Options*. Boulder, CO: Westview Press, 1993.

Khan, Akbar. *Raiders in Kashmir*. Islamabad: National Book Foundation, 1970.

Khan, Mohammad Ayub. *Friends Not Masters: A Political Autobiography*. New York: Oxford University Press, 1967.

Korbel, Josef. *Danger in Kashmir*. Princeton: Princeton University Press, 1954.

Krepon, Michael, ed. *Nuclear Risk Reduction in South Asia*. New York: Palgrave Macmillan, 2004.

Lamb, Alastair. *Crisis in Kashmir, 1947 to 1966*. London: Routledge & Kegan Paul, 1966.

———. *Kashmir: A Disputed Legacy, 1846–1990*. Karachi: Oxford University Press, 1992.

Menon, Raja. *A Nuclear Strategy for India*. New Delhi: Sage, 2000.

Misri, M. L., and M. S. Bhatt. *Poverty, Planning and Economic Change in Jammu and Kashmir*. New Delhi: Vikas, 1994.

Mullik, B. N. *My Years with Nehru: Kashmir*. New Delhi: Allied Publishers, 1971.

Musharraf, Pervez. *In the Line of Fire: A Memoir.* New York: Free Press, 2006.

Newberg, Paula R. *Double Betrayal: Repression and Insurgency in Kashmir.* Washington, DC: Carnegie Endowment for International Peace, 1995.

Perkovich, George. *India's Nuclear Bomb: The Impact on Global Proliferation.* Berkeley: University of California Press, 1999.

Puri, Balraj. *Simmering Volcano: Study of Jammu Relations with Kashmir.* New Delhi: Sterling, 1983.

———. *Kashmir towards Insurgency.* Hyderabad: Orient Longman, 1993.

Puship, P. N., and K. Warikoo, eds. *Jammu, Kashmir and Ladakh: Linguistic Predicament.* Delhi: Har-Anand Publications, 1996.

Qasim, Mir. *My Life and Times.* New Delhi: Allied, 1992.

Rahman, Mushtaqur. *Divided Kashmir: Old Problems, New Opportunities, for India, Pakistan, and the Kashmiri People.* Boulder, CO: Lynne Rienner, 1996.

Rashid, Ahmed. *Taliban: Militant Islam, Oil, and Fundamentalism in Central Asia.* New Haven: Yale University Press, 2000.

———. *Descent into Chaos: How the War against Islamic Extremism Is Being Lost in Pakistan, Afghanistan and Central Asia.* London: Allen Lane, 2008.

Rizvi, Janet. *Ladakh.* Oxford University Press, 1983.

Sagan, Scott D., and Kenneth N. Waltz. *The Spread of Nuclear Weapons: A Debate Renewed, with New Sections on India and Pakistan, Terrorism, and Missile Defense.* New York: Norton, 2003.

Sareen, Rajendra. *Pakistan: The Indian Factor.* New Delhi: Allied Publishers, 1984.

Sarila, Narendra Singh. *The Shadow of the Great Game: The Untold Story of India's Partition.* New York: Carroll & Graf, 2005.

Schofield, Victoria. *Kashmir in Conflict: India, Pakistan and the Unending War.* London: I. B. Tauris, 2003.

Sender, Henry. *The Kashmiri Pandits.* Delhi: Viking, 1988.

Singh, Jasjit. *Kargil 1999: Pakistan's Fourth War for Kashmir.* New Delhi: Knowledge Works, 1999.

Singh, Karan. *Heir Apparent: An Autobiography.* Delhi: Oxford University Press, 1982.

Singh, Tavleen. *Kashmir: A Tragedy of Errors.* New Delhi: Viking, 1995.

Sisson, Richard, and Leo Rose, eds. *War and Secession: Pakistan, India, and the Creation of Bangladesh.* Berkeley: University of California Press, 1990.

Sreedhar, ed. *Dr. A. Q. Khan on Pakistan Bomb.* New Delhi: ABC Publishing, 1987.

Srivastava, C. P. *Lal Bahadur Shastri.* Delhi: Oxford University Press, 1995.

Sundarji, General Krishnaswamy. *Blind Men of Hindoostan: Indo-Pak Nuclear War.* New Delhi: UBSPD, 1993. A "fictionalised narrative" (p. xvi).

Swarup, Devendra, and Sushil Aggarwal, eds. *The Roots of the Kashmir Problem: The Continuing Battle between Secularism and Communal Separatism.* New Delhi: M. Prakashan, 1992.

Talbott, Strobe. *Engaging India: Diplomacy, Democracy, and the Bomb.* Washington, DC: Brookings Institution, 2004.

Tellis, Ashley J., C. Fair, and J. Medby. *Limited Conflicts under the Nuclear Umbrella: Indian and Pakistan Lessons from the Kargil Crisis.* Santa Monica, CA: Rand, 2002.

Teng, Mohan K., Ram K. Bhat, and Santosh Kaul. *Kashmir: Constitutional History.* New Delhi: Light & Life Publishers, 1997.

Thomas, Raju G. C., ed. *The Roots of Conflict in South Asia.* Boulder, CO: Westview Press, 1992.

Thomas, Raju G. C., and Amit Gupta, eds. *India's Nuclear Security.* Boulder, CO: Lynne Rienner, 2000.

Wakefield, W. *History of Kashmir and Kashmiris: The Happy Valley.* 1879. Reprint, Delhi: Seema Publications, 1975.

Wani, Gull M., ed. *Kashmir: Need for Sub-Continental Political Initiative.* New Delhi: Ashish Publishing House, 1995.

Wirsing, Robert G. *India, Pakistan, and the Kashmir Dispute: On Regional Conflict and Its Resolution.* New York: St. Martin's Press, 1994.

Wolpert, Stanley. *Roots of Confrontation in South Asia: Afghanistan, Pakistan, India and the Superpowers.* New York: Oxford University Press, 1982.

———. *Jinnah of Pakistan: A Life*. New York: Oxford University Press, 1984.

———. *Zulfi Bhutto of Pakistan: His Life and Times*. New York: Oxford University Press, 1993.

———. *Nehru: A Tryst with Destiny*. New York: Oxford University Press, 1996.

———. *Shameful Flight: The Last Years of the British Empire in India*. New York: Oxford University Press, 2006.

———. *India*. 1991. 4th ed. Berkeley: University of California Press, 2009.

Zutshi, Chitralekha. *Languages of Belonging: Islam, Regional Identity, and the Making of Kashmir*. New York: Oxford University Press, 2004.

Zutshi, U.K. *Emergence of Political Awakening in Kashmir*. New Delhi: Manohar Publications, 1986.

INDEX

Page numbers in italics indicate maps.

Text:	10/15 Janson
Display:	Janson
Cartographer:	Bill Nelson
Compositor:	BookComp, Inc.
Printer and Binder:	Maple-Vail Book Manufacturing Group

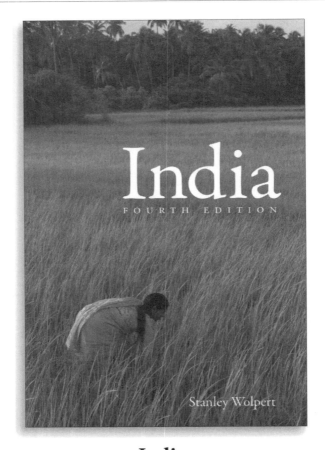

India

FOURTH EDITION

This new edition brings Stanley Wolpert's brilliantly succinct and accessible introduction to India completely up to date for a new generation of readers, travelers, and students. It includes new sections on the country's global economic development, the recent national elections, and on its international relations, including those with Pakistan, China, Sri Lanka, and the United States.   978-0-520-26032-0